Graphic Clas

MARK TWAIN

Graphic Classics Volume Eight
Second Edition
2007

Edited by Tom Pomplun

EUREKA PRODUCTIONS

8778 Oak Grove Road, Mount Horeb, Wisconsin 53572
www.graphicclassics.com

ILLUSTRATION ©2004 WILLIAM L. BROWN

Advice To Little Girls

BY MARK TWAIN

First, girls, don't smoke — that is, don't smoke to excess.
I am seventy-three and a half years old, and have been smoking
seventy-three of them. But I never smoke to excess — that is,
I smoke in moderation, only one cigar at a time.
Second, don't drink — that is, don't drink to excess.
Third, don't marry — I mean, to excess.

ILLUSTRATED BY LISA K. WEBER

ILLUSTRATION ©2004 MARK DANCEY

Graphic Classics:
MARK TWAIN

Cover illustration by George Sellas
Back cover illustration by Kevin Atkinson,
color by Steve Mannion
Additional illustrations by
William L. Brown and Mark Dancey

Graphic Classics: Mark Twain is published by Eureka Productions. ISBN:13 #978-0-9787919-2-6 / ISBN:10 #0-9787919-2-4. Second edition, 2007. Price US $11.95, CAN $14.50. Available from Eureka Productions, 8778 Oak Grove Road, Mount Horeb, WI 53572. Tom Pomplun, designer and publisher, tom@graphicclassics.com. Eileen Fitzgerald and Lisa Agnew, editorial assistants. Compilation and all original works ©2007 Eureka Productions. Graphic Classics is a trademark of Eureka Productions. For ordering information and previews of new volumes visit http://www.graphicclassics.com. Printed in Canada.

TOM SAWYER ABROAD

by MARK TWAIN

Adapted by TOM POMPLUN
Illustrated by GEORGE SELLAS

Do you reckon Tom Sawyer was satisfied after all them adventures? I mean the adventures we had down the river, and the time we set Jim free and Tom got shot in the leg. No, he wasn't. It only just p'isoned him for more.

For a while he WAS satisfied. Everybody made much of him, and he tilted up his nose and stepped around the town as though he owned it.

Well, by and by Tom's glory got to paling, on account of other things turning up for people to talk about — first a horse race, then a fire, and on top of that the eclipse; and by that time there wasn't any more talk about Tom.

So then he set to work on a plan to make him celebrated; and offered to take me and Jim in. Tom Sawyer was always free and generous that way.

WE'LL HAVE A *CRUSADE!*

WHAT'S A CRUSADE?

HUCK FINN, DO YOU MEAN TO TELL ME YOU DON'T KNOW WHAT A *CRUSADE* IS?

NO, I DON'T. AND I DON'T *CARE* TO, NUTHER.

I'VE LIVED 'TIL NOW AND DONE WITHOUT IT, AND I DON'T SEE ANY USE IN CLOGGING UP MY HEAD WITH THINGS WHEN I MAYN'T EVER HAVE ANY OCCASION TO USE 'EM.

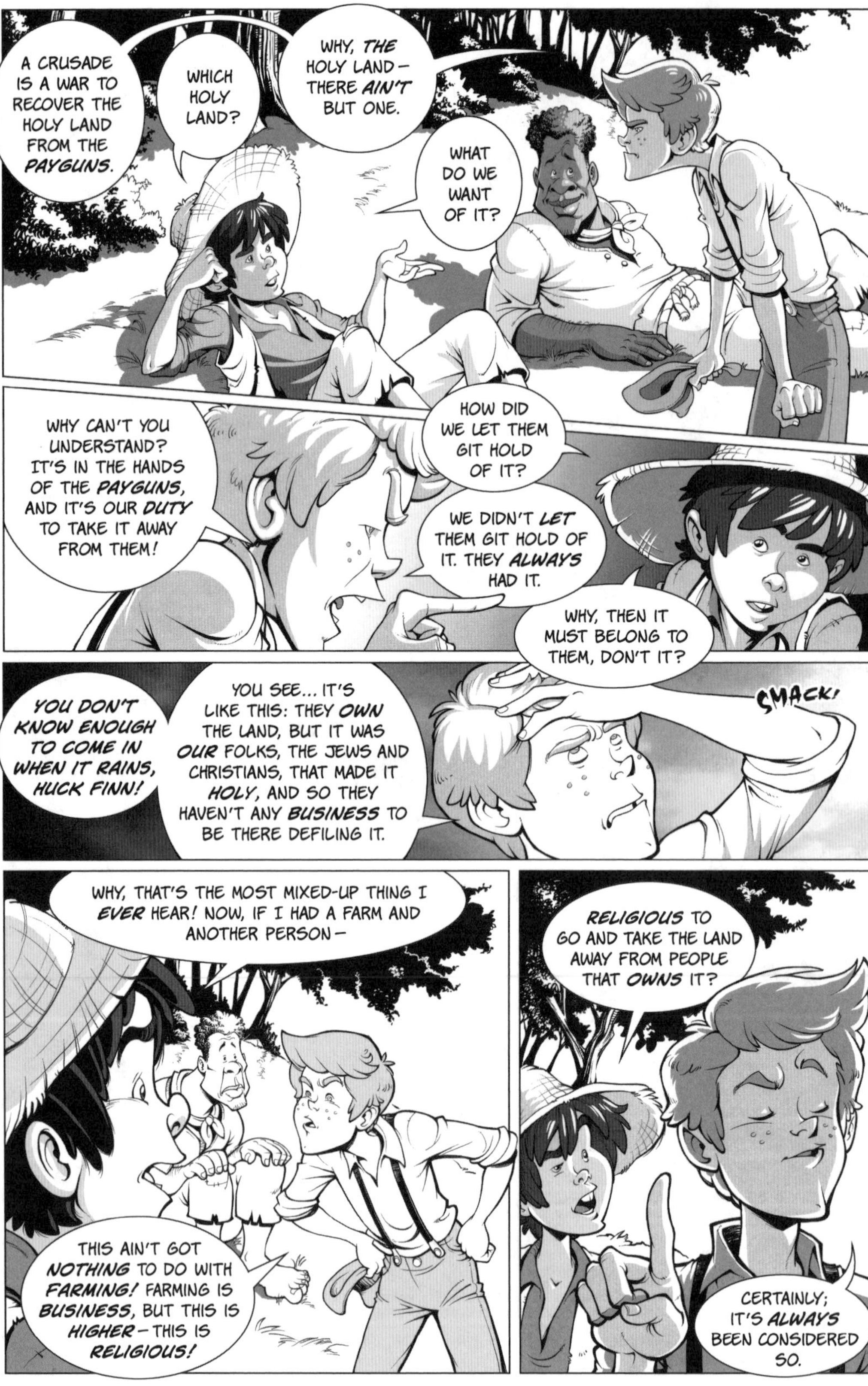
A CRUSADE IS A WAR TO RECOVER THE HOLY LAND FROM THE *PAYGUNS*.
WHICH HOLY LAND?
WHY, *THE* HOLY LAND— THERE *AIN'T* BUT ONE.
WHAT DO WE WANT OF IT?
WHY CAN'T YOU UNDERSTAND? IT'S IN THE HANDS OF THE *PAYGUNS*, AND IT'S OUR *DUTY* TO TAKE IT AWAY FROM THEM!
HOW DID WE LET THEM GIT HOLD OF IT?
WE DIDN'T *LET* THEM GIT HOLD OF IT. THEY *ALWAYS* HAD IT.
WHY, THEN IT MUST BELONG TO THEM, DON'T IT?
YOU DON'T KNOW ENOUGH TO COME IN WHEN IT RAINS, HUCK FINN!
YOU SEE... IT'S LIKE THIS: THEY *OWN* THE LAND, BUT IT WAS *OUR* FOLKS, THE JEWS AND CHRISTIANS, THAT MADE IT *HOLY*, AND SO THEY HAVEN'T ANY *BUSINESS* TO BE THERE DEFILING IT.
SMACK!
WHY, THAT'S THE MOST MIXED-UP THING I *EVER* HEAR! NOW, IF I HAD A FARM AND ANOTHER PERSON—
THIS AIN'T GOT *NOTHING* TO DO WITH *FARMING!* FARMING IS *BUSINESS*, BUT THIS IS *HIGHER*—THIS IS *RELIGIOUS!*
RELIGIOUS TO GO AND TAKE THE LAND AWAY FROM PEOPLE THAT *OWNS* IT?
CERTAINLY; IT'S *ALWAYS* BEEN CONSIDERED SO.

BUT TOM, I RECKON THERE'S A MISTAKE SOMEWHERES. I'S RELIGIOUS MYSELF, AND I KNOWS PLENTY OF RELIGIOUS PEOPLE, BUT I AIN'T RUN ACROSS *NONE* THAT ACTS LIKE *THAT*.

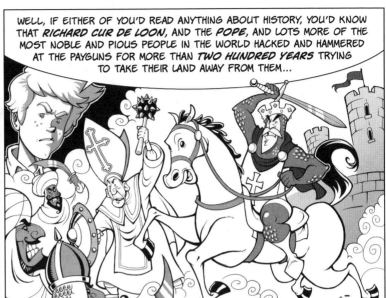

WELL, IF EITHER OF YOU'D READ ANYTHING ABOUT HISTORY, YOU'D KNOW THAT *RICHARD CUR DE LOON*, AND THE *POPE*, AND LOTS MORE OF THE MOST NOBLE AND PIOUS PEOPLE IN THE WORLD HACKED AND HAMMERED AT THE PAYGUNS FOR MORE THAN *TWO HUNDRED YEARS* TRYING TO TAKE THEIR LAND AWAY FROM THEM...

...AND YET HERE'S A COUPLE OF *SAP-HEADED COUNTRY YAHOOS* SETTING THEMSELVES UP TO KNOW MORE ABOUT THE *RIGHTS* AND *WRONGS* OF IT THAN *THEY* DID! TALK ABOUT *CHEEK!*

WELL... IF IT'S OUR *DUTY*, WE GOT TO GO AND DO THE BEST WE CAN. SAME TIME, I FEEL SORRY FOR THEM PAYGUNS. THE HARD PART'S GOIN' TO BE TO KILL FOLKS THAT AIN'T DONE US NO HARM. IF WE WAS TO GO 'MONGST 'EM, WHY, MAYBE THEY'S JUST LIKE *OTHER* PEOPLE.

I DON'T WANT TO ARGUE ANY MORE WITH PEOPLE LIKE YOU AND HUCK FINN, THAT AIN'T GOT ANY MORE SENSE THAN TO TRY TO REASON OUT A THING THAT'S PURE *THEOLOGY* BY THE LAWS THAT PROTECT *REAL ESTATE!*

He said we didn't know enough to take the chance for glory when we had it. But I didn't care much. I am peaceable, and don't get up rows with people that ain't doing nothing to me.

Well, Tom got up one new scheme after another, but they all had tender spots about 'em somewheres. So at last he was about in despair, 'til he saw something in the St. Louis papers. Tom thought he wanted to go down and see, and he wanted me and Jim to go too.

It was a big balloon, and had wings and fans and all sorts of things attached. There was a crowd around it, making fun of it, and making fun of the man.

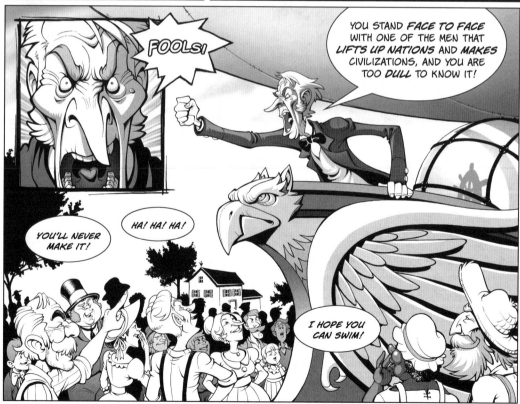

FOOLS!

YOU STAND *FACE TO FACE* WITH ONE OF THE MEN THAT *LIFTS UP NATIONS* AND *MAKES* CIVILIZATIONS, AND YOU ARE TOO *DULL* TO KNOW IT!

YOU'LL NEVER MAKE IT!

HA! HA! HA!

I HOPE YOU CAN SWIM!

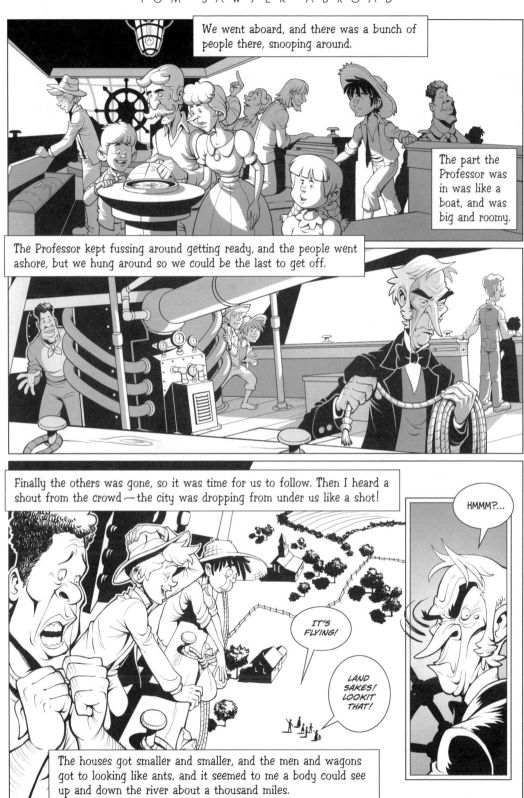

We went aboard, and there was a bunch of people there, snooping around.

The part the Professor was in was like a boat, and was big and roomy.

The Professor kept fussing around getting ready, and the people went ashore, but we hung around so we could be the last to get off.

Finally the others was gone, so it was time for us to follow. Then I heard a shout from the crowd — the city was dropping from under us like a shot!

HMMM?...

IT'S FLYING!

LAND SAKES! LOOKIT THAT!

The houses got smaller and smaller, and the men and wagons got to looking like ants, and it seemed to me a body could see up and down the river about a thousand miles.

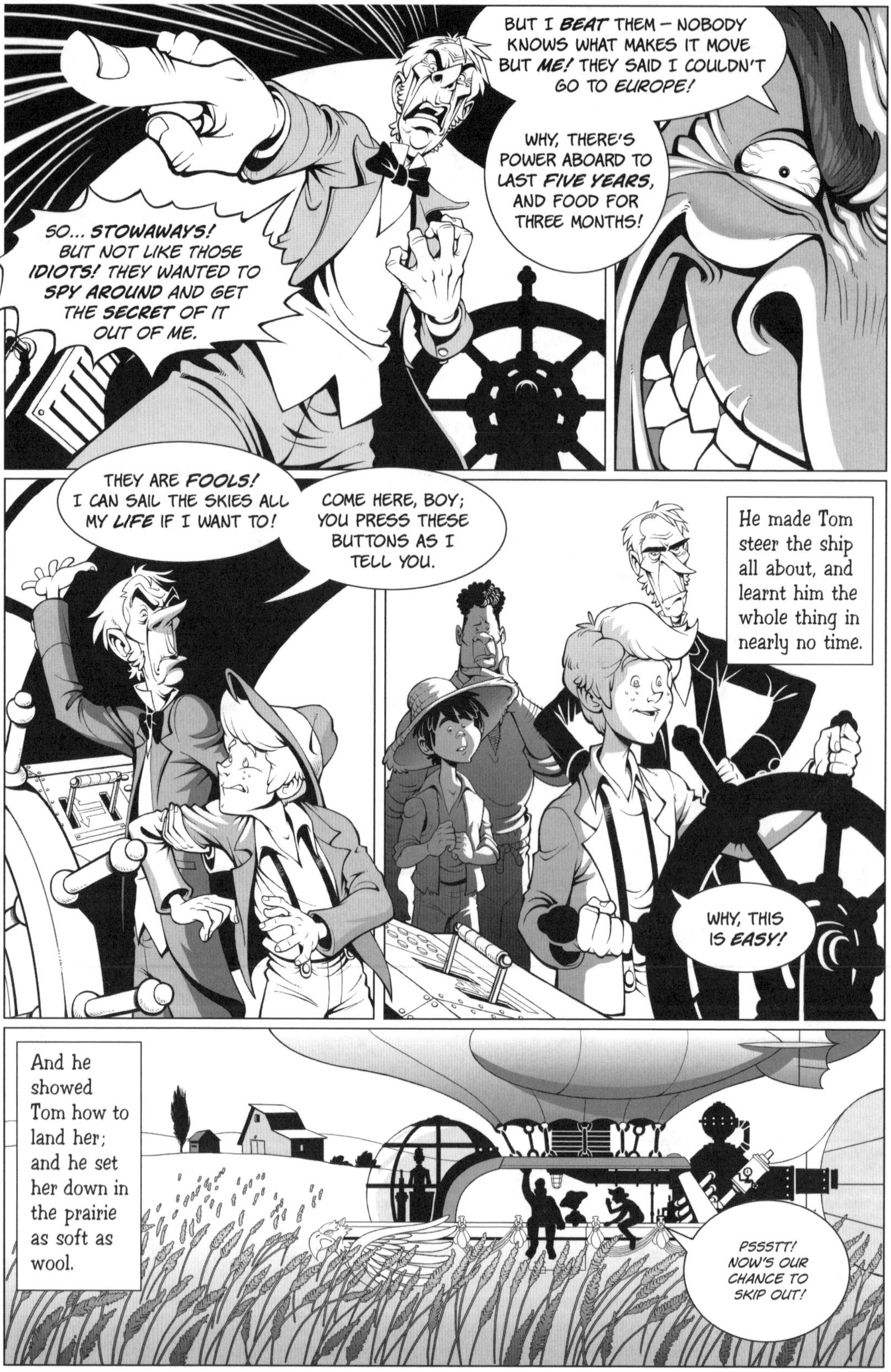
SO... STOWAWAYS! BUT NOT LIKE THOSE IDIOTS! THEY WANTED TO SPY AROUND AND GET THE SECRET OF IT OUT OF ME.
BUT I BEAT THEM – NOBODY KNOWS WHAT MAKES IT MOVE BUT ME! THEY SAID I COULDN'T GO TO EUROPE!
WHY, THERE'S POWER ABOARD TO LAST FIVE YEARS, AND FOOD FOR THREE MONTHS!
THEY ARE FOOLS! I CAN SAIL THE SKIES ALL MY LIFE IF I WANT TO!
COME HERE, BOY; YOU PRESS THESE BUTTONS AS I TELL YOU.
He made Tom steer the ship all about, and learnt him the whole thing in nearly no time.
WHY, THIS IS EASY!
And he showed Tom how to land her; and he set her down in the prairie as soft as wool.
PSSSTT! NOW'S OUR CHANCE TO SKIP OUT!

KCHAK!

WHOOOSH

NO, YOU DON'T!

WHOA!

YOU'RE *NOT* LEAVING ME! THE WORLD WILL *NEVER* GET MY SECRET! I'LL SAIL THIS BALLOON AROUND THE *GLOBE*, JUST TO SHOW WHAT IT CAN DO...

...AND THEN I'LL SINK IT IN THE SEA, AND ALL OF US WITH IT!

When night came on, he give us something to eat, and made us go to the other end of the boat, and he laid down on a locker, where he could boss all the works.

IF ANY OF YOU TRIES TO LAND HER, I'LL *KILL* HIM!

We set scrunched up together and didn't say much, we was so scared. The night dragged along slow and lonesome. The farmhouses looked snug and homeful in the moonshine, and we wished we could be down there; but we just slipped along over them like a ghost.

When we woke up in the morning, the Professor pitched us some breakfast and gave us our orders. He stood in the middle of the boat, by what he said was the midship compass.

YOU THREE STAY ABAFT OF THIS COMPASS... *OR ELSE!*

Well, when you has slept and eaten, everything looks pretty different from what it done before, even when you are up in a balloon with a crazy genius.

TOM, DIDN'T WE START *EAST?*

YES... WE DID.

AND HOW *FAST* HAVE WE BEEN GOING?

WELL, THE PROFESSOR SAID WE WAS MAKING A HUNDRED MILES AN HOUR, SOMETIMES MORE.

WELL, THEN, I RECKON THE PROFESSOR *LIED.*

WHY DO YOU SAY THAT?

BECAUSE IF WE WAS GOING SO FAST WE OUGHT TO BE PAST *ILLINOIS*, OUGHTN'T WE?

CERTAINLY.

WELL, WE *AIN'T*. YOU CAN SEE FOR YOURSELF BY THE COLOR.

WHAT'S THE *COLOR* GOT TO DO WITH IT?

IT'S GOT *EVERYTHING* TO DO WITH IT. ILLINOIS IS *GREEN*, INDIANA IS *PINK*—

I'VE SEEN IT ON THE *MAP*, AND IT'S *PINK*.

IF I WAS SUCH A *NUMBSKULL* AS *YOU*, HUCK FINN, I WOULD *JUMP OVERBOARD!* DID YOU RECKON THE STATES WAS THE SAME COLOR OUT-OF-DOORS AS THEY ARE ON THE *MAP?*

WHAT'S A MAP *FOR?* AIN'T IT TO LEARN YOU *FACTS?*

‹SIGH› OF COURSE.

WELL, THEN, HOW'S IT GOING TO DO *THAT* IF IT TELLS *LIES?*

THAT'S WHAT *I* WANT TO KNOW, TOM SAWYER!

AIN'T NO USE, TOM; HE GOT YOU *THIS* TIME!

I didn't have time to gloat, 'cause all of a sudden we see something and all jumped up to gaze.

AIN'T THAT THE — WE'RE *WAY* PAST INDIANA! IT'S THE *OCEAN!*

We all stood petrified but happy, for none of us had ever seen an ocean, or ever expected to. Then a monster city slid past underneath us, and Tom said it was New York.

WHY, IT'S JUST TOO *SPLENDID* TO BELIEVE!

Then we was over the very ocean itself, and going like a cyclone.

PLEASE SIR, TURN US AROUND!

GET BACK AND KEEP QUIET!

14

The land was gone, all but a little streak away off on the edge of the water, and under us was just ocean — heaving and pitching and squirming — the roomiest place I ever see, and the lonesomest.

THAT'S A SEXTANT. HE'S TAKING THE SUN TO SEE WHEREABOUTS THE BALLOON IS.

WE'LL KEEP UP THIS GAIT UNTIL TOMORROW AFTERNOON, THEN WE'LL LAND IN LONDON.

WE'LL BE HUMBLY THANKFUL.

SO... YOU DON'T WANT TO GO TO ENGLAND.

DON'T THINK YOU'RE GOING TO LEAVE ME!

That evening...

⟨HIC⟩ FOOLS! NOBODY KNOWS THE SECRET BUT ME. ⟨HIC⟩

HE'S GETTING DRUNK.

I DON'T LIKE THE LOOKS OF THIS.

It was dark now, and getting stormy, and the Professor went on talking to himself, getting wilder and wilder. It got so black we could hardly see him any more.

NO!

PO' TOM, HE'S A GONER!

WAIT — I SEE SOMETHING — *IT'S TOM!*

Tom clumb aboard, and when Jim found it was him, and not his ghost, he hugged him and carried on like he was gone crazy, he was so glad.

But we never see the Professor again. The storm let go about this time with all its might; and it was dreadful the way the thunder boomed and the rain come down. We huddled up in the bow, talking about the poor Professor, and how the world had made fun of him and made him go deranged.

About midnight the storm quit, so we stretched out and went to sleep. In the morning, it was nice weather, and we tried to make some plans.

LET'S TURN AROUND AND GO HOME.

I'M FOR *THAT!*

WE'RE SO FAR TOWARD ENGLAND THAT WE MIGHT AS WELL *GO* THERE, AND HAVE THE GLORY OF SAYING WE *DONE IT.*

BUT HOW DO YOU KNOW WE'RE STILL *ON COURSE?*

WELL, SHE BEEN WANDERING SINCE THE... *ACCIDENT.* SHE'S IN A WIND NOW THAT'S BLOWING HER SOUTH OF EAST...

So then he p'inted her east, and we rousted out a breakfast. We found water and food, a charcoal stove and matches, and books, maps, blankets and money, too. Tom learned me and Jim how to steer, and divided us up into four-hour watches.

Toward the middle of the afternoon we got ready to land, and we kept watching for England, but we couldn't see nothing but ocean.

The afternoon wasted out and still there warn't no land anywheres. We wondered what was the matter, but we went on steering east, and Tom got out the Professor's maps.

The next morning...

WAKE UP! IT'S LAND— GLORY BE!

Well, there was the land sure enough — as far as you could see, and perfectly level and yaller. We hunted everywheres for London, but couldn't find hair nor hide of it.

THIS AIN'T *MY* NOTION OF *ENGLAND*— I HAD THE IDEA IT LOOKED LIKE *AMERICA*.

As the sun came up the weather got to blistering. Jim settled down above the land, which wasn't anything but pure sand, and Tom and me clumb down the ladder and took a run to stretch our legs. The stretch felt amazing good, but the sand scorched our feet like hot embers.

GOLLY!

OOH! OUCH!

Then we heard a shout from Jim.

RUN! RUN FO' YO' LIVES!

IT'S LIONS! I KIN SEE 'EM THROUGH THE SPYGLASS!

We begun to heel it back to the balloon, but I was so scared it took the stiffening all out of my legs. I could only just gasp along the way you do in a dream when there's a ghost gaining on you.

Tom shinned up the ladder to the boat and shouted to Jim to soar away, but my legs shook so, I dasn't try to climb.

Jim stopped the balloon about a quarter of a mile off, and they helped me aboard. And when that gang saw we was gone they sat down on their hams and looked up at us so disappointed that it was as much as a person could do not to see their side of the matter.

HANG ON, HUCK! WE'LL GET YOU OUT OF HERE!

I KNOW WHERE WE ARE—WE'RE IN THE *GREAT SAHARA!*

WHERE'S THE GREAT SAHARA? IN *ENGLAND* OR IN *SCOTLAND?*

'TAIN'T IN *EITHER*; IT'S IN *AFRICA!*

Tom took the wheel, while Jim begun to stare down with no end of interest, because Africa was where his ancestry come from.

20

As we come down we could see the camels plodding along, an everlasting string of them, and a hundred people in long white robes, with a thing like a shawl bound over their heads.

We stopped about a hundred yards over their heads. The people set up a yell and scampered every which way, and some begun to fire their guns at us.

We see that we was making trouble, so we went up about a mile and watched them from there. It took them an hour to get together and get started again.

21

We poked along, looking down at them with the glass, and by and by we see a big sand mound, and a bunch of people on horses come tearing down it, with lances, and guns blazing.

Both sides crashed together and was all mixed up, and there was a popping of guns, and the air got so full of smoke you could only catch glimpses of them fighting.

At last the robbers see they couldn't win, so their chief sounded a signal, and all that was left of them broke away and went scampering across the plain.

HUZZAH!

The last man to go snatched up a child and carried it off. A woman run screaming after him, and we see her sink down on the sand and cover her face with her hands.

EEEEEE!

When we saw what that yahoo did, we come a-whizzing down on him.

YOU GIT THAT DEVIL, TOM!

We swooped low, and Tom knocked that villun right out of his saddle. The child fell to the sand and wasn't hurt, and the robber staggered off like he didn't know what hit him.

THWOP!

OOFGH!

GAHH!

Jim shinned down the ladder and fetched up the kid, and started for the mother. When he was close to her the child goo-goo'd, and she heard it.

She whirled and fetched a shriek of joy, and snatched the kid, then hugged Jim.

Jim, he shoved up the ladder, and in a minute we was sailing away in the sky.

YOU'RE MOS' WELCOME, MA'AM!

That night was one of the prettiest nights I ever see. We didn't want to go to sleep, and so Tom told us the stories he'd read about in the Arabian Nights.

The morning was cool, but the weather soon got to blazing, and when we went for the water, it was spoiled and pretty near hot enough to scald your mouth.

BLECCHH!

MERCY!

WE GOT TO FIND AN OASIS, OR THERE AIN'T NO TELLING WHAT WILL HAPPEN!

Two hours — three hours — and nothing but sand, sand, SAND. A body don't know what real misery is 'til he is thirsty all the way through and is certain he ain't ever going to come to water no more.

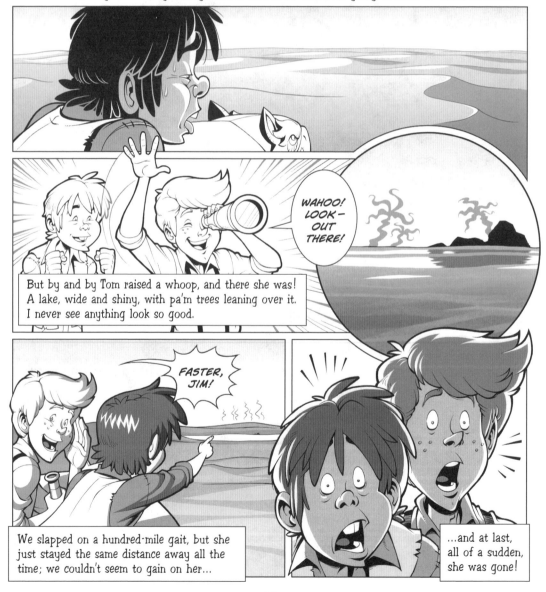

WAHOO! LOOK-OUT THERE!

But by and by Tom raised a whoop, and there she was! A lake, wide and shiny, with pa'm trees leaning over it. I never see anything look so good.

FASTER, JIM!

We slapped on a hundred-mile gait, but she just stayed the same distance away all the time; we couldn't seem to gain on her...

...and at last, all of a sudden, she was gone!

24

WHY, IT WAS JUST A *MIRODGE!*

I DON'T CARE NOTHING ABOUT ITS *NAME*, THE THING I WANT TO KNOW IS...

WHAT'S BECOME OF IT?

WHAT'S BECOME OF IT? WHY, YOU SEE YOURSELF IT'S GONE.

YES, BUT WHERE'S IT GONE *TO?*

IT AIN'T ANYTHING BUT *IMAGINATION!*

DIDN'T I SEE A LAKE, TOM SAWYER?

YES — YOU *THINK* YOU DID.

THE LAKE *WAS* THERE — I SEEN IT TOO —

FULL SPEED, JIM, DON'T YOU TAKE YOUR EYES OFF OF IT!

IT WON'T DO YOU NO GOOD — THERE *AIN'T* NO LAKE THERE.

OH, MY GOODNESS GRACIOUS, THERE IT IS AGI'N!

25

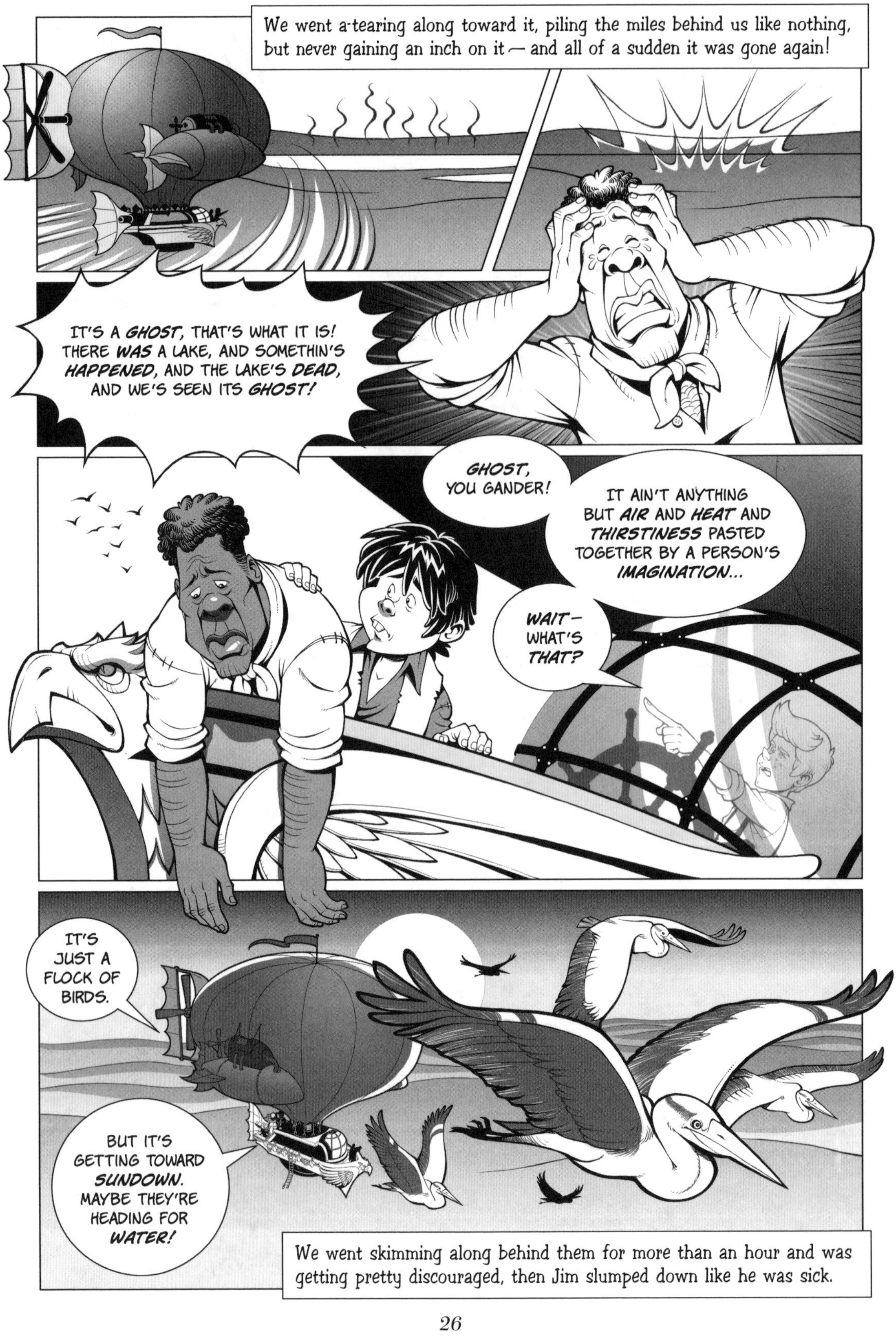
We went a-tearing along toward it, piling the miles behind us like nothing, but never gaining an inch on it — and all of a sudden it was gone again!
IT'S A *GHOST*, THAT'S WHAT IT IS! THERE *WAS* A LAKE, AND SOMETHIN'S *HAPPENED*, AND THE LAKE'S *DEAD*, AND WE'S SEEN ITS *GHOST!*
GHOST, YOU GANDER!
IT AIN'T ANYTHING BUT *AIR* AND *HEAT* AND *THIRSTINESS* PASTED TOGETHER BY A PERSON'S *IMAGINATION*...
WAIT— WHAT'S *THAT?*
IT'S JUST A FLOCK OF BIRDS.
BUT IT'S GETTING TOWARD *SUNDOWN*. MAYBE THEY'RE HEADING FOR *WATER!*
We went skimming along behind them for more than an hour and was getting pretty discouraged, then Jim slumped down like he was sick.

HUCK — THE *LAKE* — SHE'S THERE *AG'IN*, AND NOW I *KNOWS* I'S GOIN' TO *DIE*, 'CAUSE WHEN A BODY SEES A GHOST THE *THIRD* TIME, THAT'S WHAT IT MEANS.

NO! GET UP AND LOOK, YOU SAPHEADS!

We stood up, and there was the water, right under us — enough to make a body cry, it was so beautiful.

WAAAAAHOOOOOO!

We dropped anchor, then clumb down and drunk a barrel apiece, and had a fine swim. I've tasted a many a good thing in my life, but nothing half as good as that water.

We stayed there 'til morning, then filled our tank and headed east.

We went flying along for a day or two, and then we struck the east end of the desert at last. Away off on the edge of the sand, we could see three little sharp roofs like tents.

IT'S THE PYRAMIDS OF EGYPT!

That made my heart fairly jump. You see, there was a feller come to the Sunday-school once, and made a speech, and said the pyramids was five hundred foot high, all built out of hunks of stone as big as a bureau. If it hadn't been in Sunday-school, I would 'a judged it was a lie.

As we come nearer we see the sand end in a wide country of bright green, with a snaky stripe crooking through it, and Tom said it was the Nile.

And when Jim got so he could believe it WAS the land of Egypt, he wouldn't enter it standing up, because he said it wasn't fitten' for a humble man to come any other way to the land of Moses and Joseph and Pharaoh and the other prophets. He was a Presbyterian, and had a most deep respect for Moses, who was a Presbyterian, too.

Then one of them early morning fogs started up, and Jim straddled the bow to watch out for danger ahead. The fog got so solid that Jim looked dim and smoky.

OH, FOR LAND'S SAKE, SET HER BACK, TOM!

HERE'S THE BIGGEST GIANT OUTTA THE 'RABIAN NIGHTS A-COMIN' STRAIGHT FOR US!

Tom slammed on the back-action, and as we slowed to a standstill a man's face as big as a house looked in over the gunnel. Jim went over backwards into the boat and I about laid down and died.

HE AIN'T ALIVE, YOU FOOLS; IT'S THE SPHINX!

The fog cleared, and we stood off a piece, and sailed around it, and it was just grand. It was a man's head on a lion's body, and there was a little temple between its front paws.

We landed Jim on top of the head with an American flag to protect him, it being a foreign land; then we backed off to git what Tom called perspective, while Jim struck different kinds of attitudes and positions.

Then we sailed off further, 'til we couldn't hardly see Jim anymore, and then that great figger was at its noblest, a-gazing out over the Nile Valley so solemn and lonesome.

We set there a-looking and a-thinking for near half an hour, then at last when I looked back at the Sphinx I saw something scurrying around on its back.

TOM, WHAT'S THOSE LITTLE BLACK THINGS? THEY LOOK LIKE BUGS.

NO, THEY'RE MEN... AND THERE'S SOME PUFFS OF SMOKE... IT'S *GUNS!* *HUCK, THEY'RE AFTER JIM!*

We clapped on the power, and come a-whizzing down towards them, and they broke and scattered every which way.

We found Jim laying face down on top of the head, scared and tuckered out. They had shot at him, but the bullets couldn't git at him when he was hunkered down.

YOU HAD THE *FLAG!* WHY DIN'T YOU JUST COMMAND THEM TO *GIT*, IN THE NAME OF THE UNITED STATES?

I *DONE* IT, TOM, BUT THEY NEVER PAID NO *ATTENTION*.

WELL, I'LL JUST HAVE THIS THING LOOKED INTO AT *WASHINGTON!*

YOU'LL SEE THAT THEY'LL HAVE TO *APOLOGIZE* FOR INSULTING THE FLAG, AND PAY AN *INDEMNITY*, TOO!

WHAT'S A *INDEMNITY*, TOM?

IT'S *CASH*, THAT'S WHAT IT IS.

WHO *GITS* IT?

WHY, *WE DO*.

HOW MUCH MONEY WILL IT BE, TOM?

WELL... IN AN AGGRAVATED CASE LIKE THIS ONE, IT WILL BE AT LEAST THREE DOLLARS APIECE, MAYBE MORE.

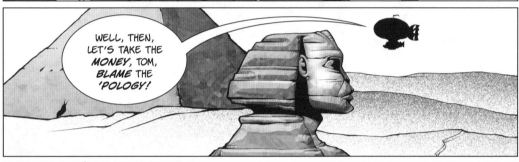

WELL, THEN, LET'S TAKE THE *MONEY*, TOM, *BLAME* THE 'POLOGY!

We left Jim to hover the ship a ways off, while Tom and me clumb down and walked up towards the pyramids to investigate.

We got near the biggest one, and found it was just like what the man said in the Sunday-school. It was like four pairs of stairs that starts broad at the bottom and slants up and comes together in a point at the top, only each step was as high as your chin.

32

We joined in with some Arabs and we clumb up to the hole where you go into the tunnel that goes to the middle of the pyramid.

Finally we came to a room with a big stone box in it where they used to keep a king. But I didn't take no interest in the place, because I thought there could be ghosts there.

After we quit the pyramid, we paid a man with some of the coins we found on the ship and rented two little donkeys. We rode a piece, then took a ferry, then rode on into the big city called Cairo.

The road was as smooth and beautiful a road as ever I see, and had tall date-pa'ms on both sides, and people and children everywhere.

And the city was a curiosity. Such narrow streets crowded with people with turbans, and women with veils — a perfect jam, and everybody noisy.

The stores warn't big enough to turn around in, but you didn't have to go in; the storekeeper sat on his counter, smoking his snaky long pipe, and had his things where he could reach them.

There was a church, where you have to take off your shoes when you go in. I never see such a big church in my life before; it made you dizzy to look up; our village church at home ain't a circumstance to it.

There was crowds of men and boys in the church, setting in groups on the stone floor and making no end of noise — getting their lessons by heart, Tom said, out of the Koran, which they think is a Bible.

They was all Moslems, Tom said, and when I asked him what a Moslem was, he said it was a person that wasn't a Presbyterian. So there is plenty of them in Missouri, though I didn't know it before.

We didn't see half there was to see in Cairo, but we thought we should get back to the balloon 'fore dark.

When we got back there was a young man there that could talk English and wanted to hire to us as a guide.

So we hired him and took him on board. We piled on the power, and by the time we was through dinner we was over the place where the Israelites crossed the Red Sea.

Jim said he could see it all now, just the way it happened.

THERE'S THE ISRAELITES WALKING ALONG BETWEEN THE WALLS OF WATER...

...AND THE EGYPTIANS COMING AFTER THEM, AND THE WALLS TUMBLIN' TOGETHER, DROWNIN' THE LAST MAN OF 'EM.

Then we flew over Mount Sinai, and saw where Moses broke the tables of stone, and where the children of Israel worshiped the golden calf, and the guide knowed the place as well as I knowed the village at home.

But then we had an accident, and it fetched all the plans to a standstill: Tom's ornery corn-cob pipe had got so old that she caved in and went to pieces.

Tom, he didn't know WHAT to do. The professor's pipe wouldn't answer; it warn't anything but a mershum, and he wouldn't take mine. So there we was.

Tom thought it over, and said we must scour around and see if we could roust out a cob pipe in Egypt or Arabia, but the guide said it warn't no use; they didn't have them.

So Tom was pretty glum for a little while, but then he chirked up and said he knowed what to do.

I'VE GOT *ANOTHER* CORN-COB PIPE BACK *HOME*. IT'S LAYING ON THE RAFTER THAT'S RIGHT OVER THE KITCHEN STOVE.

JIM, YOU AND THE GUIDE WILL GO AND GET IT, AND ME AND HUCK WILL CAMP HERE ON MOUNT SINAI 'TIL YOU COME BACK!

BUT *TOM*, I COULDN'T *EVER* FIND OUR VILLAGE, NOR ST. LOUIS, NOR EVEN *AMERICA — I DON'T KNOW THE WAY!*

GULP!

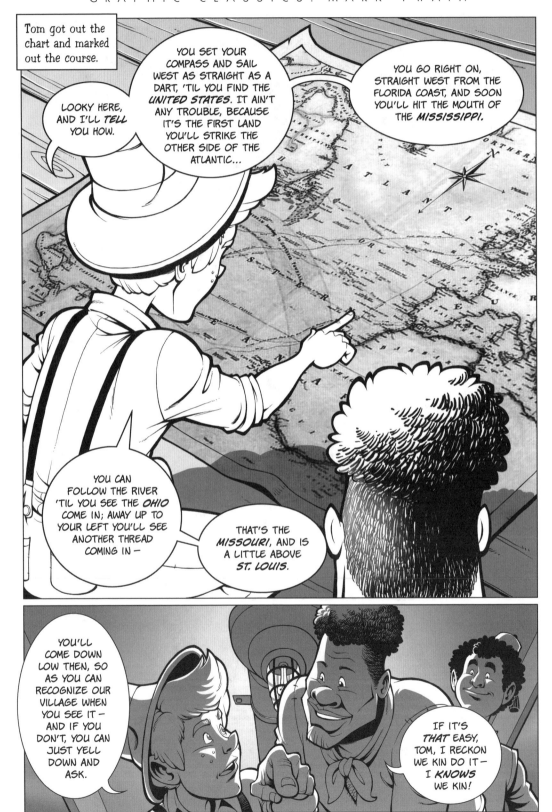

Tom got out the chart and marked out the course.

LOOKY HERE, AND I'LL *TELL* YOU HOW.

YOU SET YOUR COMPASS AND SAIL WEST AS STRAIGHT AS A DART, 'TIL YOU FIND THE *UNITED STATES*. IT AIN'T ANY TROUBLE, BECAUSE IT'S THE FIRST LAND YOU'LL STRIKE THE OTHER SIDE OF THE ATLANTIC...

YOU GO RIGHT ON, STRAIGHT WEST FROM THE FLORIDA COAST, AND SOON YOU'LL HIT THE MOUTH OF THE *MISSISSIPPI*.

YOU CAN FOLLOW THE RIVER 'TIL YOU SEE THE *OHIO* COME IN; AWAY UP TO YOUR LEFT YOU'LL SEE ANOTHER THREAD COMING IN —

THAT'S THE *MISSOURI*, AND IS A LITTLE ABOVE *ST. LOUIS*.

YOU'LL COME DOWN LOW THEN, SO AS YOU CAN RECOGNIZE OUR VILLAGE WHEN YOU SEE IT — AND IF YOU DON'T, YOU CAN JUST YELL DOWN AND ASK.

IF IT'S *THAT* EASY, TOM, I RECKON WE KIN DO IT — I *KNOWS* WE KIN!

IT'S ONLY ABOUT SEVEN THOUSAND MILES.

LAND A LITTLE BACK OF THE THE WOODS, OUT OF SIGHT; THEN JIM, YOU SLIP IN THE BACK WAY TO THE KITCHEN AND GIT THE PIPE, AND LAY THIS PIECE OF PAPER ON THE KITCHEN TABLE.

AT THREE HUNDRED MILES AN HOUR YOU CAN MAKE THE TRIP IN A DAY EACH WAY.

Tom Sawyer the Erronort sends his love to Aunt Polly from Mount Sinai, in Egypt, and so does Huck Finn.
Tom Sawyer
the Erronort

Tom and me hustled out some blankets and food and things, then Jim landed us on top of the mountain.

THIS IS *THURSDAY*; YOU'LL BE BACK HERE SATURDAY AFTERNOON. I WANT A *SMOKE*, AND THE QUICKER YOU FETCH THAT PIPE, THE *BETTER*.

IN TWENTY-FOUR HOURS YOU'LL BE HOME, AND IT'LL BE EARLY MORNING, VILLAGE TIME. JUST DON'T LET *AUNT POLLY*, NOR NOBODY ELSE CATCH SIGHT OF YOU!

She seemed to whiz out of sight in a second. We found a comfortable cave that looked out over the whole plain, and there we camped to wait for the pipe.

Two days later the balloon come back right on time; but Aunt Polly had catched Jim when he was getting the pipe, and anybody can guess what happened.

TOM, SHE'S OUT ON THE *PORCH* WITH HER *EYE* SET ON THE SKY, A-LAYIN' FOR YOU...

AND SHE SAY SHE AIN'T GOIN' TO *BUDGE* FROM THERE 'TIL SHE GITS HOLD OF YOU!

THERE'S GOIN' TO BE *TROUBLE*, TOM SAWYER, 'DEED THERE IS.

THE END

The Celebrated Jumping Frog of Calaveras County

IN COMPLIANCE WITH THE REQUEST OF A FRIEND OF MINE, I CALLED ON GARRULOUS OLD **SIMON WHEELER**, AND INQUIRED AFTER THE **REV. LEONIDAS W. SMILEY.**

I FOUND SIMON WHEELER DOZING COMFORTABLY BY THE BAR-ROOM STOVE OF THE DILAPIDATED TAVERN IN THE ANCIENT MINING CAMP OF ANGEL'S. HE ROUSED UP AND GAVE ME A GOOD DAY. I TOLD HIM A FRIEND OF MINE HAD COMMISSIONED ME TO MAKE SOME INQUIRIES ABOUT A COMPANION OF HIS BOYHOOD NAMED LEONIDAS W. SMILEY- A YOUNG MINISTER OF THE GOSPEL, WHO HE HAD HEARD WAS A RESIDENT OF ANGEL'S CAMP.

ADAPTED & ILLUSTRATED BY KEVIN ATKINSON

SIMON WHEELER BACKED ME INTO A CORNER AND BLOCKADED ME THERE WITH HIS CHAIR, AND THEN SAT ME DOWN AND REELED OFF THE FOLLOWING NARRATIVE:

THERE WAS A FELLER HERE ONCE BY THE NAME OF **JIM SMILEY**, IN THE WINTER OF '49...

"...OR MAYBE IT WAS THE SPRING OF '50 — I DON'T RECALL EXACTLY, BUT ANY WAY, HE WAS THE CURIOUSEST MAN ABOUT ALWAYS BETTING ON ANYTHING YOU EVER SEE, IF HE COULD GET ANY BODY TO BET ON THE OTHER SIDE. AND IF HE COULDN'T, HE'D CHANGE SIDES. ANY WAY THAT SUITED THE OTHER MAN WOULD SUIT HIM."

"BUT STILL, HE WAS UNCOMMON LUCKY; HE MOST ALWAYS COME OUT A WINNER."

"JUST SO HE GOT A BET, HE WAS SATISFIED."

"THERE COULDN'T BE NO SOLIT'RY THING MENTIONED BUT THAT FELLER'D OFFER TO BET ON IT."

"IF THERE WAS A HORSE RACE, YOU'D FIND HIM FLUSH..."

"...OR YOU'D FIND HIM BUSTED AT THE END OF IT."

"IF THERE WAS A CAT FIGHT, HE'D BET ON IT."

"IF THERE WAS A CHICKEN FIGHT, HE'D BET ON IT."

"WHY, IF THERE WAS TWO BIRDS SETTIN' ON A FENCE HE WOULD BET YOU WHICH ONE WOULD FLY FIRST."

"PARSON WALKER'S WIFE LAY SICK ONCE, AND IT SEEMED AS IF THEY WARN'T GOING TO SAVE HER; BUT ONE MORNING HE COME IN, AND SMILEY ASKED HOW SHE WAS, AND HE SAID SHE WAS CONSIDERABLE BETTER AND WITH THE BLESSING OF PROV'DENCE SHE'D GET WELL YET; AND SMILEY, BEFORE HE THOUGHT SAYS..."

WELL, I'LL RISK TWO-AND-A-HALF SHE **DON'T**, ANYWAY.

"THISH-YER SMILEY HAD A MARE - THE BOYS CALLED HER THE FIFTEEN-MINUTE NAG, BUT THAT WAS ONLY IN FUN, BECAUSE, OF COURSE, SHE WAS FASTER THAN THAT - AND HE USED TO WIN MONEY ON THAT HORSE, FOR ALL SHE WAS SO SLOW AND ALWAYS HAD THE ASTHMA, OR THE DISTEMPER, OR THE CONSUMPTION OR SOMETHING OF THAT KIND. "

"THEY USED TO GIVE HER THREE HUNDRED YARDS START, AND THEN PASS HER UNDERWAY; BUT ALWAYS AT THE FAG-END OF THE RACE SHE'D GET EXCITED, AND COME CAVORTING UP, AND KICKING UP M-O-R-E DUST AND RAISING M-O-R-E RACKET WITH HER COUGHING AND SNEEZING AND BLOWING HER NOSE - AND ALWAYS FETCH UP AT THE STAND JUST ABOUT A NECK AHEAD."

"AND HE HAD A LITTLE BULL PUP, THAT TO LOOK AT HIM YOU'D THINK HE WARN'T WORTH A CENT, BUT TO SET AROUND AND LOOK ORNERY. "

" BUT AS SOON AS MONEY WAS UP ON HIM, HE WAS A DIFFERENT DOG; HIS TEETH WOULD UNCOVER AND SHINE SAVAGE."

"AND A DOG MIGHT TACKLE HIM, AND BITE HIM, AND THROW HIM OVER HIS SHOULDER TWO OR THREE TIMES, AND ANDREW JACKSON—WHICH WAS THE NAME OF THE PUP- ANDREW JACKSON WOULD NEVER LET ON BUT WHAT HE WAS SATISFIED, AND HADN'T EXPECTED NOTHING ELSE- AND THE BETS BEING DOUBLED ON THE OTHER SIDE ALL THE TIME, TILL THE MONEY WAS ALL UP; AND THEN ALL OF THE SUDDEN HE WOULD GRAB THAT OTHER DOG BY THE J'INT OF HIS HIND LEG AND JEST HANG ON TILL THEY THREW UP THE SPONGE, IF IT WAS A YEAR."

"HE GAVE SMILEY A LOOK, AS MUCH TO SAY HIS HEART WAS BROKE, AND IT WAS HIS FAULT FOR PUTTING UP A DOG THAT HADN'T NO LEGS FOR HIM TO TAKE HOLT OF WHICH WAS HIS MAIN DEPENDENCE IN A FIGHT."

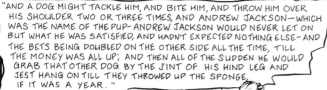

"SMILEY ALWAYS COME OUT A WINNER ON THAT PUP, TILL HE HARNESSED A DOG ONCE THAT DIDN'T HAVE NO HIND LEGS, BECAUSE THEY'D BEEN SAWED OFF BY A CIRCULAR SAW, AND WHEN THE THING HAD GONE FAR ENOUGH AND THE MONEY WAS ALL UP, AND HE COME TO MAKE A SNATCH FOR HIS PET HOLT, HE SAW IN A MINUTE HOW HE'D BEEN IMPOSED ON, AND HE DIDN'T TRY NO MORE TO WIN THE FIGHT, AND SO HE GOT SHUCKED OUT BAD."

"AND THEN HE LIMPED OFF A PIECE AND LAID DOWN AND DIED."

"IT WAS A GOOD PUP, THAT ANDREW JACKSON. IT ALWAYS MAKES ME FEEL SORRY WHEN I THINK OF THAT LAST FIGHT OF HIS'N AND THE WAY IT TURNED OUT."

"WELL, THISH-YER SMILEY HAD RAT-TARRIERS, AND CHICKEN COCKS, AND TOM-CATS, AND ALL THEM KIND OF THINGS, AND YOU COULDN'T FETCH NOTHING FOR HIM TO BET ON BUT HE'D MATCH YOU."

"AND SO HE NEVER DONE NOTHING FOR THREE MONTHS BUT SET IN HIS BACK YARD AND LEARN THAT FROG TO JUMP."

"HE KETCHED A FROG ONE DAY, AND TOOK HIM HOME, AND SAID HE CAL'KLATED TO EDERCATE HIM."

"AND YOU BET HE DID LEARN HIM, TOO, HE'D GIVE HIM A LITTLE PUNCH BEHIND, AND THE NEXT MINUTE YOU'D SEE HIM WHIRLING IN THE AIR AND COME DOWN FLAT-FOOTED LIKE A CAT. DAN'L WEBSTER WAS THE NAME OF THE FROG, AND WHEN IT COME TO JUMPING ON A LEVEL, HE COULD GET OVER MORE GROUND AT ONE STRADDLE THAN ANY ANIMAL OF HIS BREED YOU EVER SEE."

"SMILEY WAS MONSTROUS PROUD OF HIS FROG, AS WELL HE MIGHT BE, FOR FELLERS THAT HAD TRAVELED AND BEEN EVERYWHERES, ALL SAID HE LAID OVER ANY FROG THEY EVER SEE."

"WELL, SMILEY KEPT THE BEAST IN A LITTLE LATTICE BOX, AND HE USED TO FETCH HIM DOWN TOWN SOMETIMES AND LAY FOR A BET. ONE DAY A FELLER—A STRANGER IN THE CAMP—COME ACROSS HIM WITH HIS BOX AND SAYS:"

WHAT MIGHT IT BE THAT YOU'VE GOT IN THE BOX?

IT MIGHT BE A PARROT OR IT MIGHT BE A CANARY, MAY BE, BUT IT AN'T—IT'S ONLY JUST A FROG.

"AND THE FELLER LOOKED AT IT CAREFUL AND SAYS..."

H'M—SO 'TIS... WELL, WHAT'S HE GOOD FOR?

HE'S GOOD FOR ONE THING...

...HE CAN OUT JUMP ANY FROG IN CALAVERAS COUNTY.

"THE FELLER TOOK THE BOX AGAIN, AND TOOK ANOTHER LONG, PARTICULAR LOOK, AND GIVE IT BACK TO SMILEY AND SAYS VERY DELIBERATE..."

WELL, I DON'T SEE NO P'NTS ABOUT THAT FROG THAT'S ANY BETTER 'N' ANY OTHER FROG.

MAY BE YOU DON'T. MAY BE YOU UNDERSTAND FROGS, AND MAY BE YOU DON'T UNDERSTAND 'EM.

ANYWAYS I'VE GOT MY OPINION AND I'LL RISK FORTY DOLLARS THAT SAYS HE CAN OUT-JUMP ANY FROG IN CALAVERAS COUNTY.

"THEN THE FELLER SAYS, KINDA SAD LIKE..."

WELL, I'M ONLY A STRANGER HERE, AND I AN'T GOT NO FROG; BUT IF I HAD A FROG, I'D BET YOU.

THAT'S ALL RIGHT—THAT'S ALL RIGHT—IF YOU HOLD MY BOX A MINUTE, I'LL GO GET YOU A FROG.

"AND SO THE FELLER TOOK THE BOX AND SET DOWN TO WAIT."

"HE SAT THERE A GOOD WHILE THINKING TO HISSELF, AND THEN HE GOT THE FROG OUT AND PRIZED HIS MOUTH OPEN AND TOOK A TEASPOON AND FILLED HIM FULL OF QUAIL SHOT- FILLED HIM PRETTY NEAR UP TO HIS CHIN..."

"...AND SET HIM ON THE FLOOR."

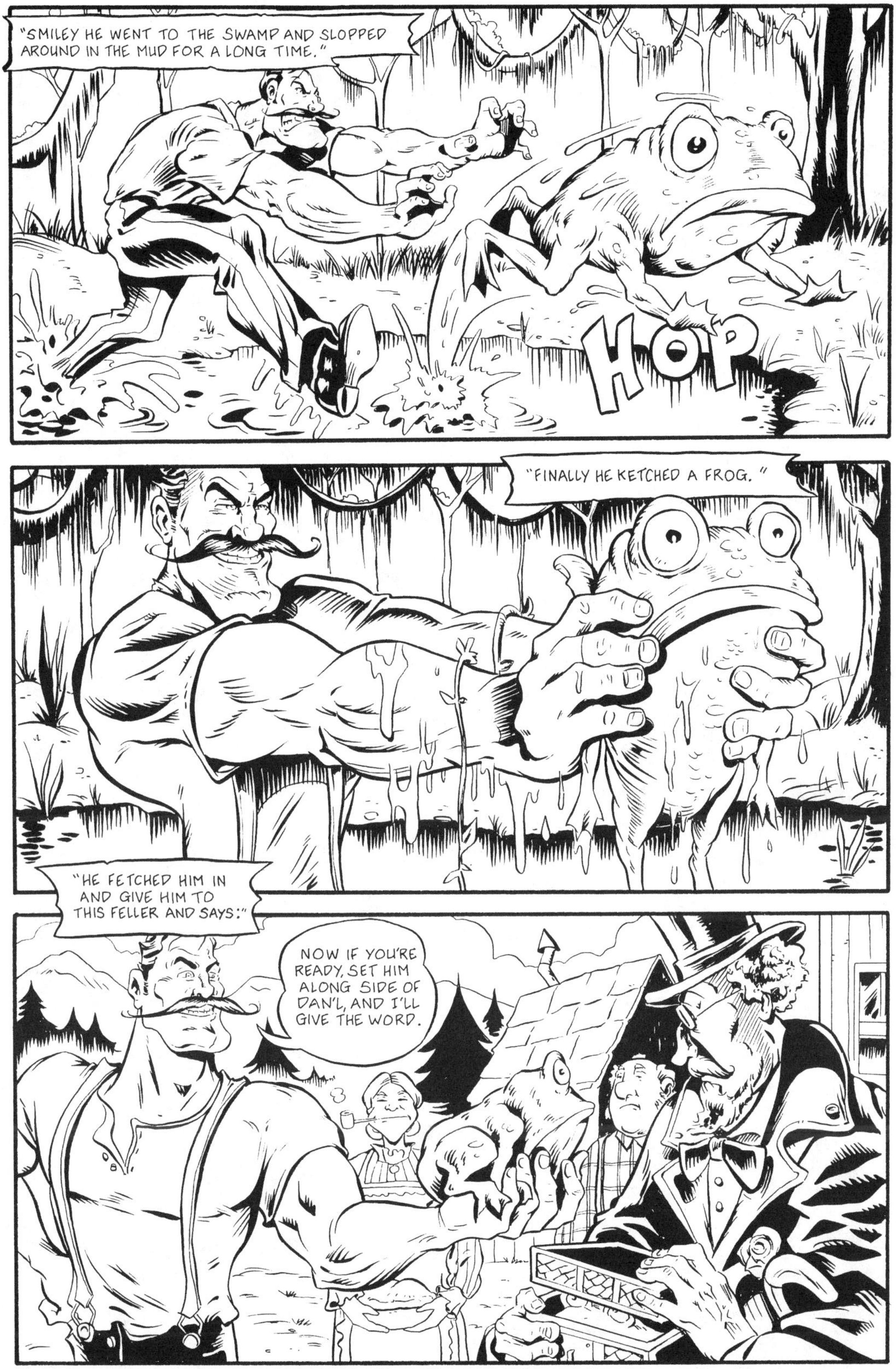
"SMILEY HE WENT TO THE SWAMP AND SLOPPED AROUND IN THE MUD FOR A LONG TIME."
HOP
"FINALLY HE KETCHED A FROG."
"HE FETCHED HIM IN AND GIVE HIM TO THIS FELLER AND SAYS:"
NOW IF YOU'RE READY, SET HIM ALONG SIDE OF DAN'L, AND I'LL GIVE THE WORD.

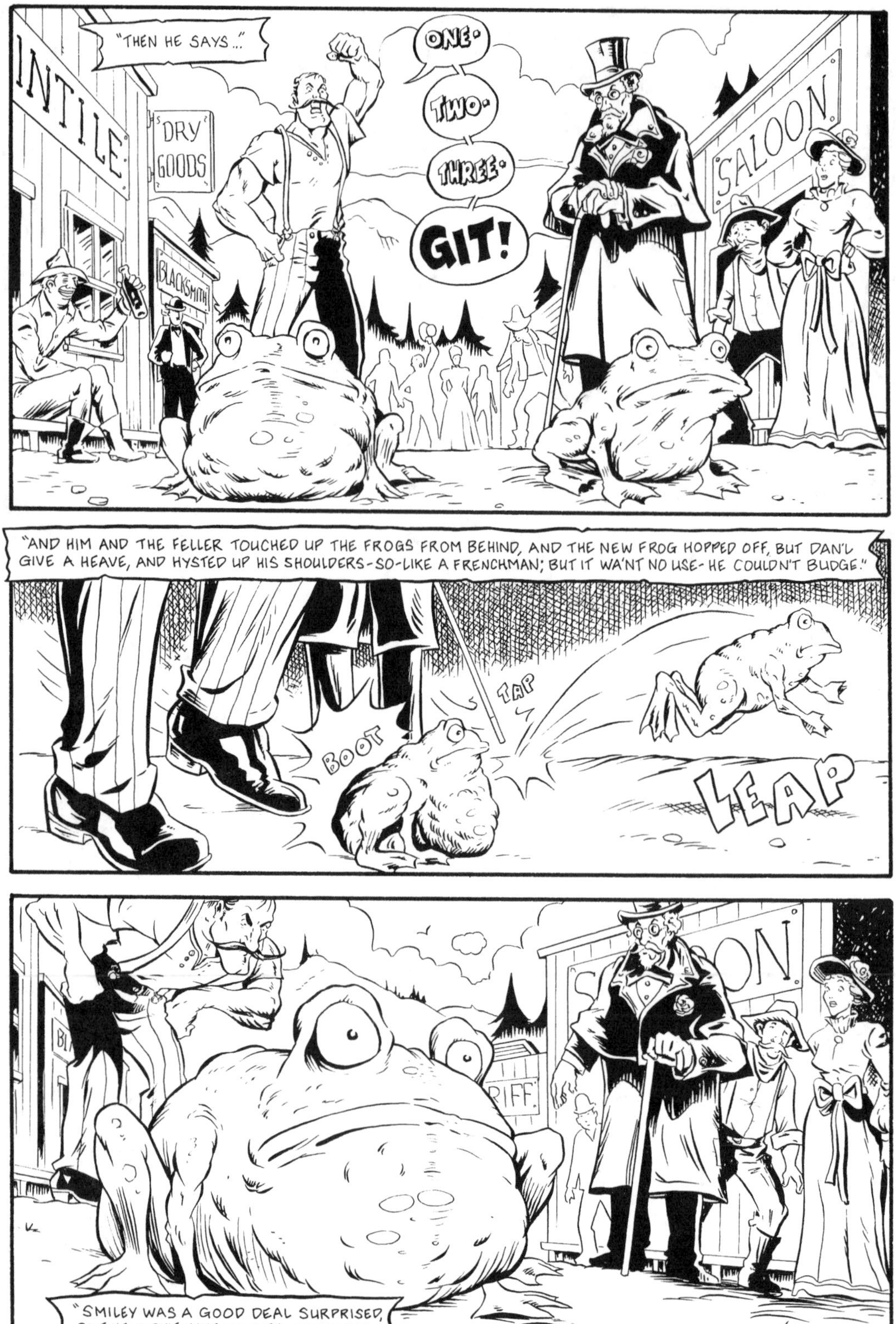
"THEN HE SAYS..."
DRY GOODS
BLACKSMITH
SALOON
ONE-
TWO-
THREE-
GIT!
"AND HIM AND THE FELLER TOUCHED UP THE FROGS FROM BEHIND, AND THE NEW FROG HOPPED OFF, BUT DAN'L GIVE A HEAVE, AND HYSTED UP HIS SHOULDERS-SO-LIKE A FRENCHMAN; BUT IT WA'NT NO USE- HE COULDN'T BUDGE."
TAP
BOOT
LEAP
"SMILEY WAS A GOOD DEAL SURPRISED, BUT HE DIDN'T HAVE NO IDEA WHAT THE MATTER WAS, OF COURSE."

"THE FELLER TOOK THE MONEY AND STARTED AWAY, AND SORTA JERKED HIS THUMB AT DAN'L AND SAYS..."

WELL, I DON'T SEE NO P'INTS ABOUT THAT FROG THAT'S ANY BETTER'N ANY OTHER FROG.

"SMILEY SCRATCHES HIS HEAD AND LOOKING DOWN AT DAN'L SAYS..."

I WONDER IF THERE AN'T SOMETHIN THE MATTER WITH THIS FROG?

HE 'PEARS TO LOOK MIGHTY BAGGY, SOME-HOW.

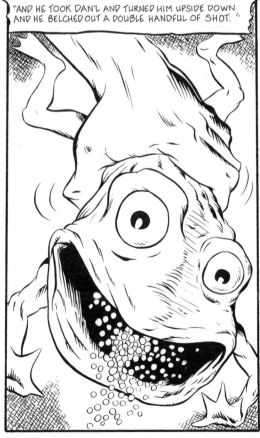

"AND HE TOOK DAN'L AND TURNED HIM UPSIDE DOWN AND HE BELCHED OUT A DOUBLE HANDFUL OF SHOT. "

"AND THEN HE SEE HOW IT WAS..."

"HE TOOK OUT AFTER THAT FELLER, BUT HE NEVER KETCHED HIM. AND —"

BUT I DID NOT THINK THAT A CONTINUATION OF THE HISTORY OF JIM SMILEY WOULD BE LIKELY TO AFFORD ME MUCH INFORMATION CONCERNING THE REV. LEONIDAS W. SMILEY, AND SO I STARTED AWAY.

TAVERN

WELL, THISH-YER SMILEY HAD A YALLER ONE-EYED COW THAT DIDN'T HAVE NO TAIL, ONLY JEST A SHORT STUMP LIKE A BANNANNER, AND —

"OH, HANG SMILEY AND HIS AFFLICTED COW!" I MUTTERED AND BIDDING THE OLD GENTLEMAN A GOOD DAY, I DEPARTED.

My father was a St. Bernard, my mother was a collie, but I am a Presbyterian. This is what my mother told me. To me they are only fine large words meaning nothing. My mother had a fondness for such.

The
UHURU-KAI
(Free-Life)
FAMILY THEATRE
presents:
A DOG'S
TALE
by Mark Twain
(Samuel Clemens)

She was of a rather vain and frivolous character; still, she had a kind heart and gentle ways, and never harbored resentments for injuries done her, and she taught her children her kindly way.

From her we learned also to be brave in time of danger, and help the best we could without stopping to think what the cost might be to us. And she taught us not by words only, but by example. So, as you see, there was more to her than her education.

When I was well grown, at last, I was sold and taken away, and I never saw her again. She was broken-hearted, and so was I, and we cried; but she comforted me as well as she could, and said we were sent into this world for a wise and good purpose, and must do our duties without repining, take our life as we might find it, live it for the best good of others, and never mind about the results.

She said men who did like this would have a beautiful reward in another world, and although we animals would not go there, to do right would give to our brief lives a dignity which in itself would be a reward. She had gathered these things when she had gone to the Sunday school with the children.

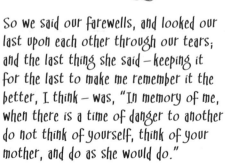

So we said our farewells, and looked our last upon each other through our tears; and the last thing she said — keeping it for the last to make me remember it the better, I think — was, "In memory of me, when there is a time of danger to another do not think of yourself, think of your mother, and do as she would do."

Do you think I could forget that? — No.

My new home was a fine house, with pictures, and rich furniture, and a great garden with spacious grounds around it. And I was the same as a member of the family, and they loved me.

Mrs. Gray was thirty, and sweet and lovely; and Sadie was ten, a darling little copy of her mother, and the baby was a year old, and never could get enough of hauling on my tail, and hugging me. Mr. Gray was thirty-eight, and tall, handsome and unsentimental.

He was a renowned scientist. I do not know what the word means, but my mother would know how to use it and get effects.

But that is not the best word; the best one was laboratory. The laboratory was filled with bottles, and electrics, and strange machines; and every week other scientists came there and made what they called experiments and discoveries.

Often I came there, and listened and tried to learn, for the sake of my mother. Other times I lay on the floor in the mistress's workroom and slept, and other times I watched by the crib in the nursery, or romped through the garden with Sadie, then slumbered while she read her book.

Still other times I went visiting among the neighbor dogs – for there were some most pleasant ones not far away, and one very handsome and courteous Irish setter who was a Presbyterian like me, and belonged to the Scotch minister.

And so, as you see, mine was a pleasant life. There could not be a happier dog than I was, nor a gratefuler one. I tried in all ways to do well and right, and honor my mother's memory and her teachings, and earn the happiness that had come to me, as best I could.

By and by came my little puppy, and then my cup was full, my happiness was perfect.

It was the dearest little waddling thing, and so smooth and soft and velvety, and had such cunning little awkward paws, and such affectionate eyes, and such a sweet and innocent face; and it made me so proud to see how the children and their mother adored it, and fondled it, and exclaimed over every little wonderful thing it did.

It did seem to me that life was just too lovely.

Then came the winter.

One day I was standing watch in the nursery...

The baby was asleep in the crib, which was next to the fireplace. A spark from the wood-fire shot out and it set the crib ablaze. A scream from the baby awoke me, and before I could think, I sprang half-way to the door.

But in the next second my mother's farewell was sounding in my ears, and I was back by the crib. I reached my head through the flames and dragged the baby out by the waist-band, and tugged it along, and we fell to the floor together in a cloud of smoke.

I dragged the screaming little creature out the door and around the bend of the hall, and was still tugging away, all happy and proud, when the master's voice shouted:

BEGONE, YOU CURSED BEAST!

He struck furiously at me with his cane, and a blow fell upon my left foreleg, which made me shriek and fall. The cane went up for another blow, but never descended, for the nurse's voice rang wildly, "The nursery's on fire!" and the master rushed away in that direction, and my other bones were saved.

The pain was cruel, but he might come back at any moment; so I limped on three legs to the other end of the hall, where there was a dark stairway leading up into a garret where people seldom went. I managed to climb up there, then I searched my way through the dark among the piles of things, and hid in the secretest place I could find.

I was so afraid that I hardly even whimpered. For half an hour there was a commotion downstairs, and then there was quiet again.

But then came a sound that froze me. They were calling my name – hunting for me!

It was the most dreadful sound that I had ever heard. It went through all the rooms, then outside, then all about the house again, and I thought it would never stop. But at last it did, hours after the twilight of the garret had been blotted out by darkness.

Then in that blessed stillness my terrors fell little by little away, and I could think out a plan now. I would creep down the back stairs, and hide behind the cellar door, and slip out and escape when the iceman came at dawn; then I would hide all day, and start on my journey when night came; to where they would not know me and betray me to the master.

I was feeling almost cheerful now; then suddenly I thought: Why, what would life be without my puppy!

That was despair. There was no plan for me; I saw that I must stay where I was, and wait, and take what might come. Then the calling began again! All my sorrows came back. I said to myself, the master will never forgive. I did not know what I had done to make him so bitter, yet I judged it was something a dog could not understand, but which was clear to a man and dreadful.

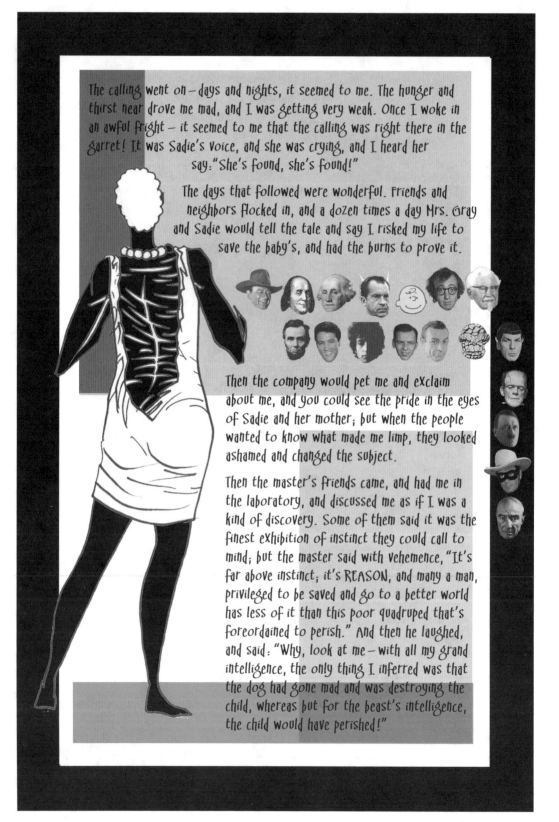

The calling went on — days and nights, it seemed to me. The hunger and thirst near drove me mad, and I was getting very weak. Once I woke in an awful fright — it seemed to me that the calling was right there in the garret! It was Sadie's voice, and she was crying, and I heard her say: "She's found, she's found!"

The days that followed were wonderful. Friends and neighbors flocked in, and a dozen times a day Mrs. Gray and Sadie would tell the tale and say I risked my life to save the baby's, and had the burns to prove it.

Then the company would pet me and exclaim about me, and you could see the pride in the eyes of Sadie and her mother; but when the people wanted to know what made me limp, they looked ashamed and changed the subject.

Then the master's friends came, and had me in the laboratory, and discussed me as if I was a kind of discovery. Some of them said it was the finest exhibition of instinct they could call to mind; but the master said with vehemence, "It's far above instinct; it's REASON, and many a man, privileged to be saved and go to a better world has less of it than this poor quadruped that's foreordained to perish." And then he laughed, and said: "Why, look at me — with all my grand intelligence, the only thing I inferred was that the dog had gone mad and was destroying the child, whereas but for the beast's intelligence, the child would have perished!"

They disputed and disputed, and I was the very center of it all, and I wished my mother could know that this grand honor had come to me; it would have made her proud. Then they discussed optics, as they called it, and whether a certain injury to the brain would produce blindness or not, but they could not agree about it, and said they must test it by experiment. Next they discussed plants, and that interested me, because in the summer Sadie and I had planted seeds—I helped her dig the holes—and after days and days a little flower came up there, and it was a wonder how that could happen, but it did. I wished I could talk—I would have told those people about it—but I didn't care for the optics; it was dull, and when they came back to it again I went to sleep.

Pretty soon it was spring, and the mother and the children went away to visit their kin. And one day those men came again and said, now for the test, and they took the puppy to the laboratory, and I limped along, feeling proud.

They discussed and experimented, until suddenly the puppy shrieked, and they set him on the floor, and he went staggering around, with his head all bloody, and the master clapped his hands and shouted:

I'VE WON! HE'S BLIND AS A BAT!

And they all said: "It's so—you've proved your theory," and they crowded around and wrung his hand.

I ran to my little darling, and snuggled close to it, and licked the blood, and it put its head against mine, whimpering softly. Then its little nose rested upon the floor, and it did not move any more.

Soon the master stopped discussing a moment, and rang in the footman, and said, "Bury it in the far corner of the garden," and then went on with the discussion. I trotted after the footman, very grateful, for I knew the puppy was out of its pain now, because it was asleep.

We went far down the garden, and there the footman dug a hole. I saw he was going to plant the puppy, and I was glad, because it would grow and come up a fine handsome dog, like his father.

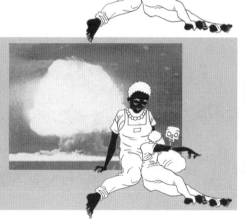

When the footman had finished and covered my little one up, he patted my head, and there were tears in his eyes, and he said:

"Poor little doggie, you saved HIS child!"

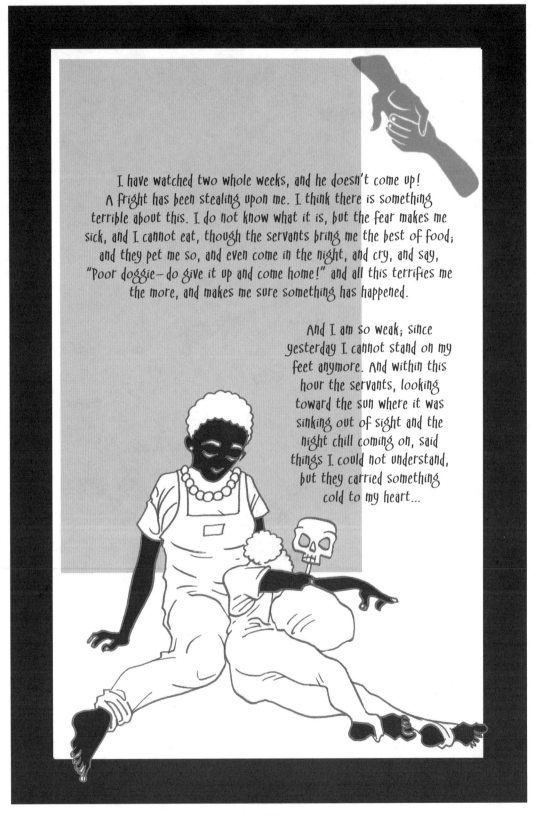

I have watched two whole weeks, and he doesn't come up!
A fright has been stealing upon me. I think there is something
terrible about this. I do not know what it is, but the fear makes me
sick, and I cannot eat, though the servants bring me the best of food;
and they pet me so, and even come in the night, and cry, and say,
"Poor doggie—do give it up and come home!" and all this terrifies me
the more, and makes me sure something has happened.

And I am so weak; since
yesterday I cannot stand on my
feet anymore. And within this
hour the servants, looking
toward the sun where it was
sinking out of sight and the
night chill coming on, said
things I could not understand,
but they carried something
cold to my heart...

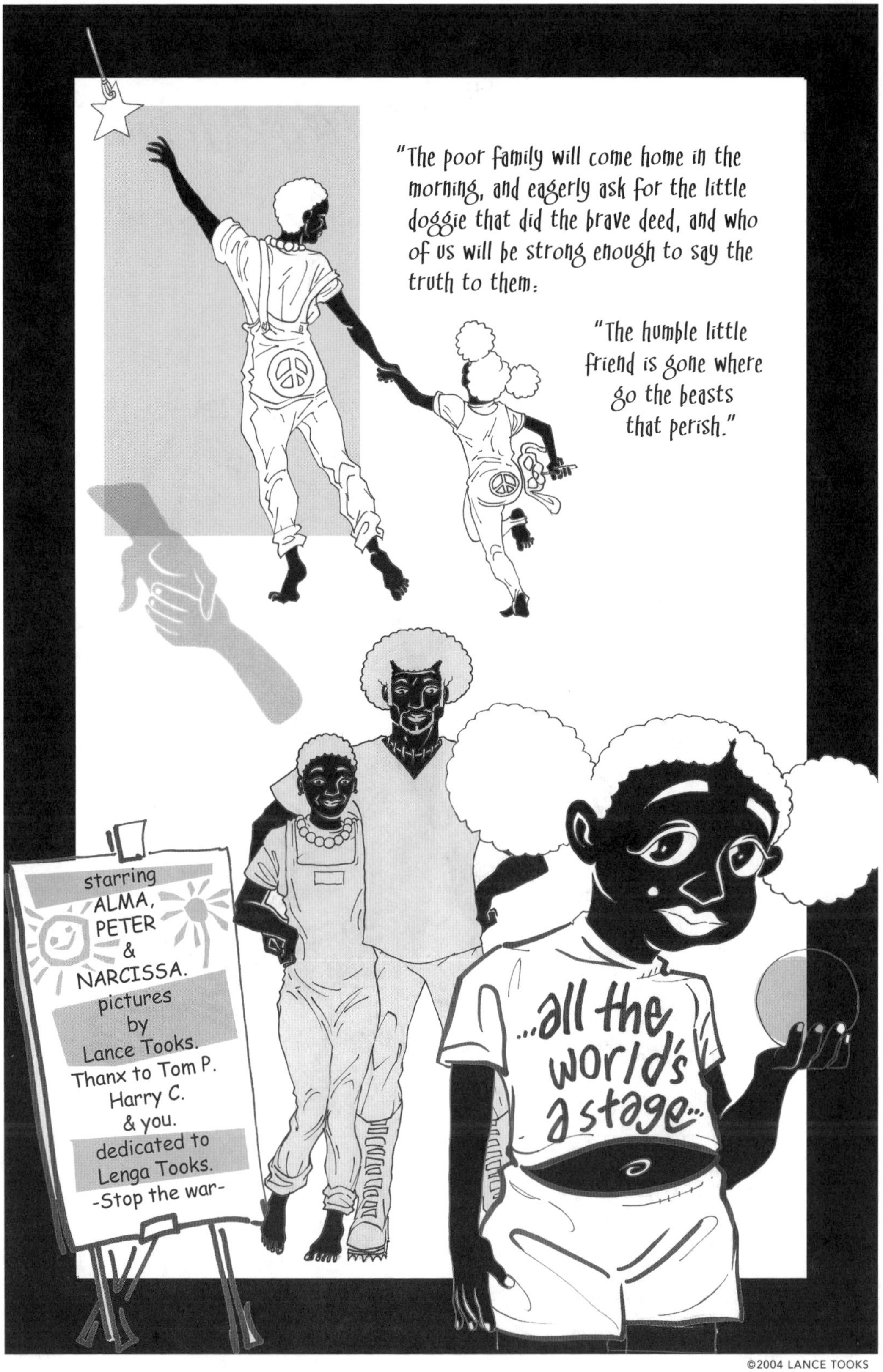
"The poor family will come home in the morning, and eagerly ask for the little doggie that did the brave deed, and who of us will be strong enough to say the truth to them:
"The humble little friend is gone where go the beasts that perish."
starring ALMA, PETER & NARCISSA. pictures by Lance Tooks. Thanx to Tom P. Harry C. & you. dedicated to Lenga Tooks. -Stop the war-
...all the world's a stage...

Advice To Little Girls

BY MARK TWAIN

Good little girls always show marked deference for the aged.
You ought never to sass old people
unless they sass you first.

ILLUSTRATED BY FLORENCE CESTAC

Good little girls *ought not to make mouths at their teachers for every trifling offense. This retaliation should only be resorted to under peculiarly aggravated circumstances.*

ILLUSTRATED BY **KIRSTEN ULVE**

If your mother *tells you to do a thing,*
it is wrong to reply that you won't. It is better and more
becoming to intimate that you will do as she bids you, and then
afterward act quietly in the matter according to the dictates of
your best judgment.

ILLUSTRATED BY **SHARY FLENNIKEN**

If you have nothing *but a rag-doll stuffed with sawdust, while one of your more fortunate little playmates has a costly China one, you should treat her with a show of kindness nevertheless. And you ought not to attempt to make a forcible swap with her unless your conscience would justify you in it, and you know you are able to do it.*

ILLUSTRATED BY **TONI PAWLOWSKY**

If at any time you find it necessary to correct your brother,
do not correct him with mud —never, on any account, throw mud
at him, because it will spoil his clothes. It is better to scald him a
little, for then you obtain desirable results. You secure his immediate
attention to the lessons you are inculcating, and at the same time
your hot water will have a tendency to move impurities from his
person, and possibly the skin, in spots.

ILLUSTRATED BY **MARY FLEENER**

You ought never *to take your little brother's chewing-gum away from him by main force; it is better to rope him in with the promise of the first two dollars and a half you find floating down the river on a grindstone. In the artless simplicity natural to this time of life, he will regard it as a perfectly fair transaction. In all ages of the world this eminently plausible fiction has lured the obtuse infant to financial ruin and disaster.*

ILLUSTRATED BY **ANNIE OWENS**

You should ever bear in mind *that it is to your kind parents that you are indebted for your food, and for the privilege of staying home from school when you let on that you are sick. Therefore you ought to respect their little prejudices, and humor their little whims, and put up with their little foibles until they get to crowding you too much.*

ILLUSTRATED BY **LESLEY REPPETEAUX**

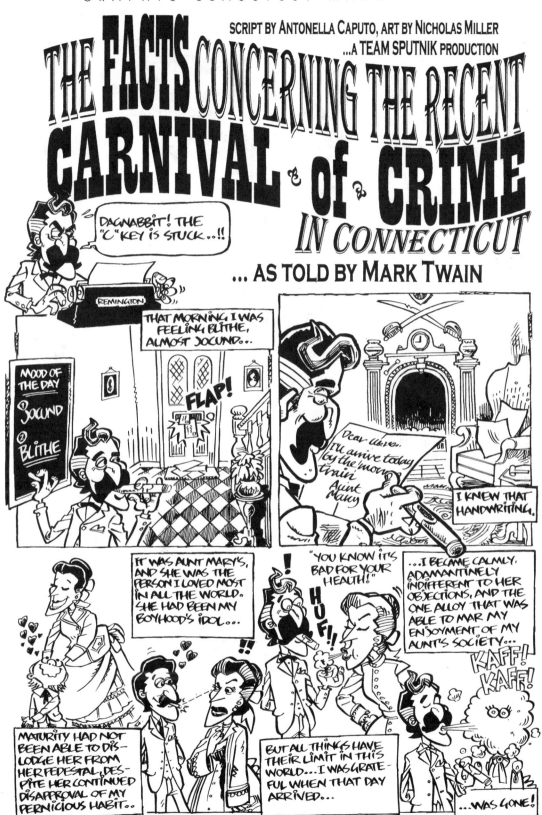

SCRIPT BY ANTONELLA CAPUTO, ART BY NICHOLAS MILLER
...A TEAM SPUTNIK PRODUCTION

THE FACTS CONCERNING THE RECENT CARNIVAL of CRIME IN CONNECTICUT

... AS TOLD BY MARK TWAIN

DAGNABBIT! THE "C" KEY IS STUCK..!!

THAT MORNING I WAS FEELING BLITHE, ALMOST JOCUND...

MOOD OF THE DAY
① JOCUND
② BLITHE

FLAP!

REMINGTON

Dear Uleve,
I'll arrive today by the morning train
Aunt Mary

I KNEW THAT HANDWRITING.

IT WAS AUNT MARY'S, AND SHE WAS THE PERSON I LOVED MOST IN ALL THE WORLD. SHE HAD BEEN MY BOYHOOD'S IDOL...

"YOU KNOW IT'S BAD FOR YOUR HEALTH!"

HUF!!

...I BECAME CALMLY, ADAMANTINELY INDIFFERENT TO HER OBJECTIONS, AND THE ONE ALLOY THAT WAS ABLE TO MAR MY ENJOYMENT OF MY AUNT'S SOCIETY...

KAFF! KAFF!

MATURITY HAD NOT BEEN ABLE TO DIS-LODGE HER FROM HER PEDESTAL, DES-PITE HER CONTINUED DISAPPROVAL OF MY PERNICIOUS HABIT...

BUT ALL THINGS HAVE THEIR LIMIT IN THIS WORLD...I WAS GRATE-FUL WHEN THAT DAY ARRIVED...

...WAS GONE!

75

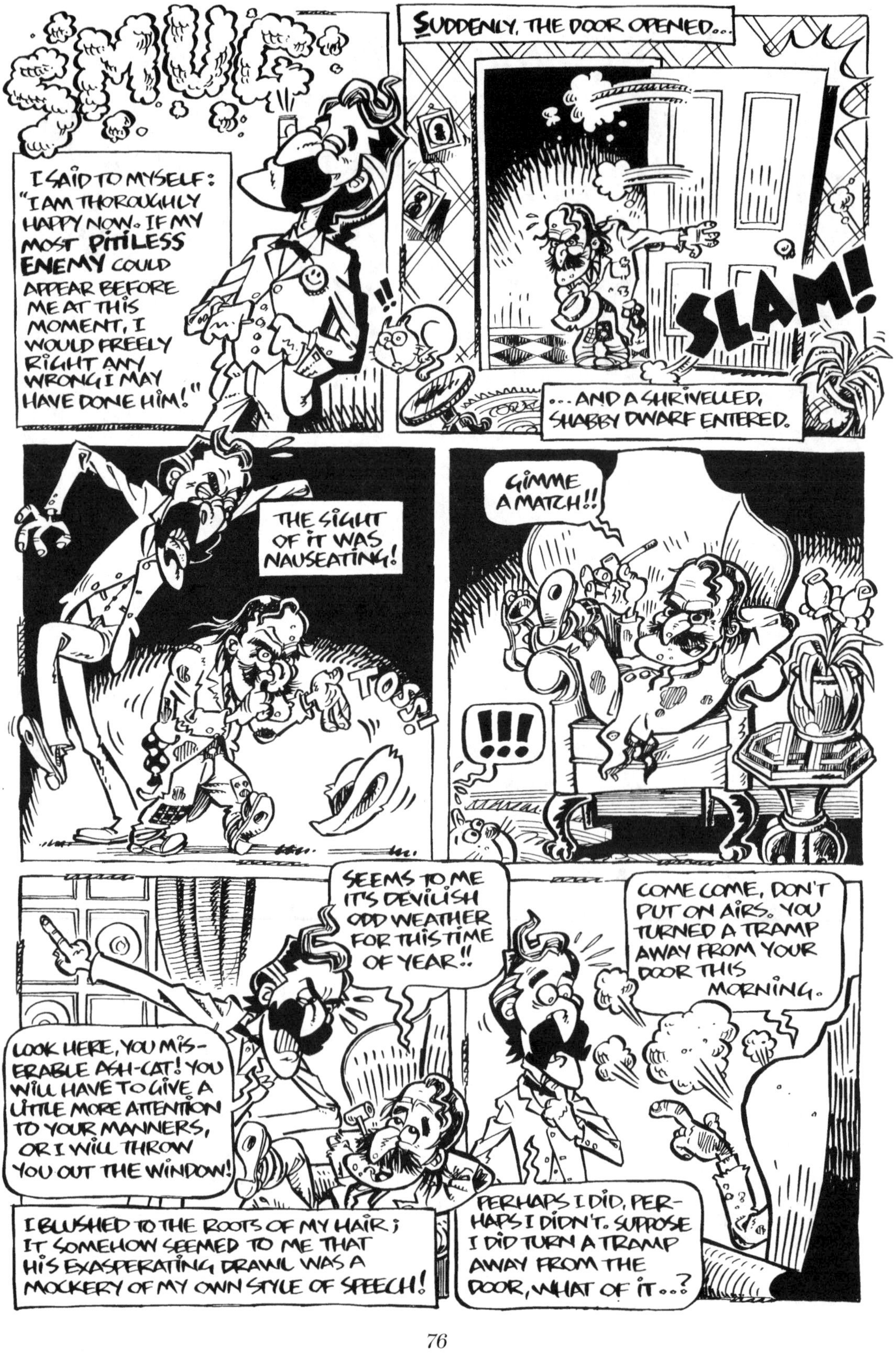
SMUG
I SAID TO MYSELF: "I AM THOROUGHLY HAPPY NOW. IF MY MOST PITILESS ENEMY COULD APPEAR BEFORE ME AT THIS MOMENT, I WOULD FREELY RIGHT ANY WRONG I MAY HAVE DONE HIM!"
!!
SUDDENLY, THE DOOR OPENED...
SLAM!
...AND A SHRIVELLED, SHABBY DWARF ENTERED.
THE SIGHT OF IT WAS NAUSEATING!
TOSS!
GIMME A MATCH!!
!!!
SEEMS TO ME IT'S DEVILISH ODD WEATHER FOR THIS TIME OF YEAR!!
LOOK HERE, YOU MISERABLE ASH-CAT! YOU WILL HAVE TO GIVE A LITTLE MORE ATTENTION TO YOUR MANNERS, OR I WILL THROW YOU OUT THE WINDOW!
I BLUSHED TO THE ROOTS OF MY HAIR; IT SOMEHOW SEEMED TO ME THAT HIS EXASPERATING DRAWL WAS A MOCKERY OF MY OWN STYLE OF SPEECH!
COME COME, DON'T PUT ON AIRS. YOU TURNED A TRAMP AWAY FROM YOUR DOOR THIS MORNING.
PERHAPS I DID, PERHAPS I DIDN'T. SUPPOSE I DID TURN A TRAMP AWAY FROM THE DOOR, WHAT OF IT...?

YOU DID, YOU LIED TO HIM!

I SAID TO THE TRAMP...

"I'M SORRY, BUT THERE IS NOTHING LEFT FROM BREAKFAST AND THE COOK HAS GONE DOWNTOWN!"

SO YOU LIED TO HIM...!!

DO YOU WANT TO HAVE TO TALK ABOUT THAT POOR YOUNG WOMAN THE OTHER DAY? IT WAS RATHER **SMALL** OF YOU TO REFUSE TO READ HER MANUSCRIPT. SHE HAD COME SO FAR, TOO, AND SO HOPEFULLY. AHA! YOU FEEL ASHAMED OF IT NOW!

I TOLD THE GIRL, IN THE **KINDEST** AND **GENTLEST** WAY, THAT I COULD NOT CONSENT TO DELIVER JUDGEMENT ON ANY-ONE'S MANUSCRIPT...

LOOK HERE, HAVE YOU ANYTHING BETTER TO DO THAN TO PRY INTO OTHER PEOPLE'S BUSINESS? DID THE GIRL TELL YOU THAT..?

DIDDA BOM DIDDA BOM...

"I SAID THE GREAT PUBLIC WAS THE ONLY TRIBUNAL COMPETENT, AND THEREFORE IT MUST BE BEST TO LAY IT BEFORE THE TRIBUNAL AT THE OUTSET."

REMORSE! REMORSE! IT SEEMED TO ME THAT IT WOULD EAT THE VERY HEART OUT OF ME...!!

REMORSE! CHOMP!

SO YOU DID, YOU SAID ALL THAT... WHEN YOU SAW THE GLADNESS GO OUT OF HER EYES AND THE TEARS BEGIN... SO ASHAMED OF HER SCRIBBLING NOW, SO PROUD OF IT BEFORE...

OH PEACE! PEACE!! THESE THOUGHTS TORTURED ME ENOUGH WITHOUT YOUR COMING HERE TO FETCH THEM BACK AGAIN..!!

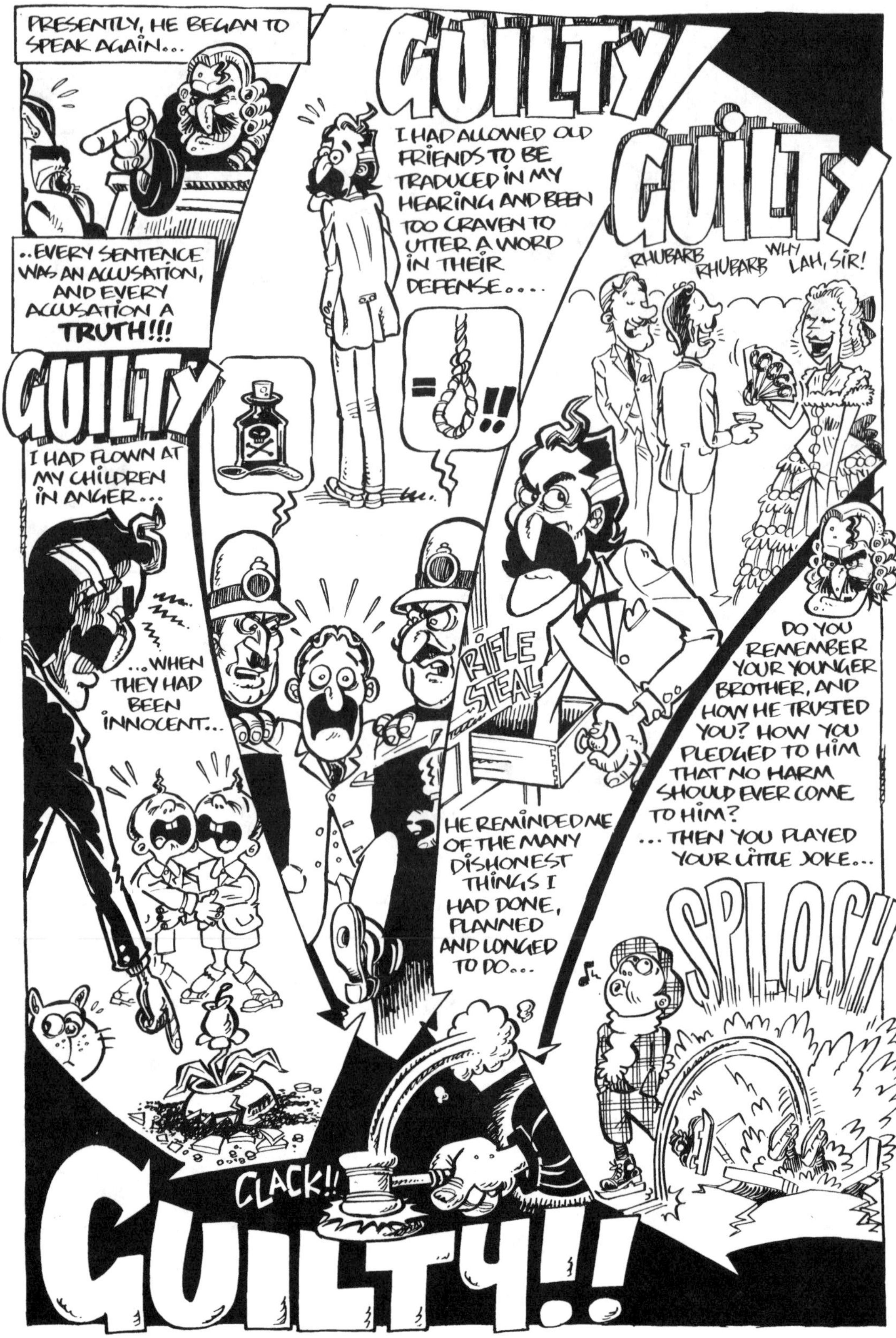
PRESENTLY, HE BEGAN TO SPEAK AGAIN...
..EVERY SENTENCE WAS AN ACCUSATION, AND EVERY ACCUSATION A TRUTH!!!
GUILTY
I HAD FLOWN AT MY CHILDREN IN ANGER...
...WHEN THEY HAD BEEN INNOCENT...
GUILTY!
I HAD ALLOWED OLD FRIENDS TO BE TRADUCED IN MY HEARING AND BEEN TOO CRAVEN TO UTTER A WORD IN THEIR DEFENSE...
GUILTY
RHUBARB RHUBARB
WHY LAH, SIR!
RIFLE STEAL!
HE REMINDED ME OF THE MANY DISHONEST THINGS I HAD DONE, PLANNED AND LONGED TO DO...
DO YOU REMEMBER YOUR YOUNGER BROTHER, AND HOW HE TRUSTED YOU? HOW YOU PLEDGED TO HIM THAT NO HARM SHOULD EVER COME TO HIM?
...THEN YOU PLAYED YOUR LITTLE JOKE...
SPLOSH
CLACK!!
GUILTY!!

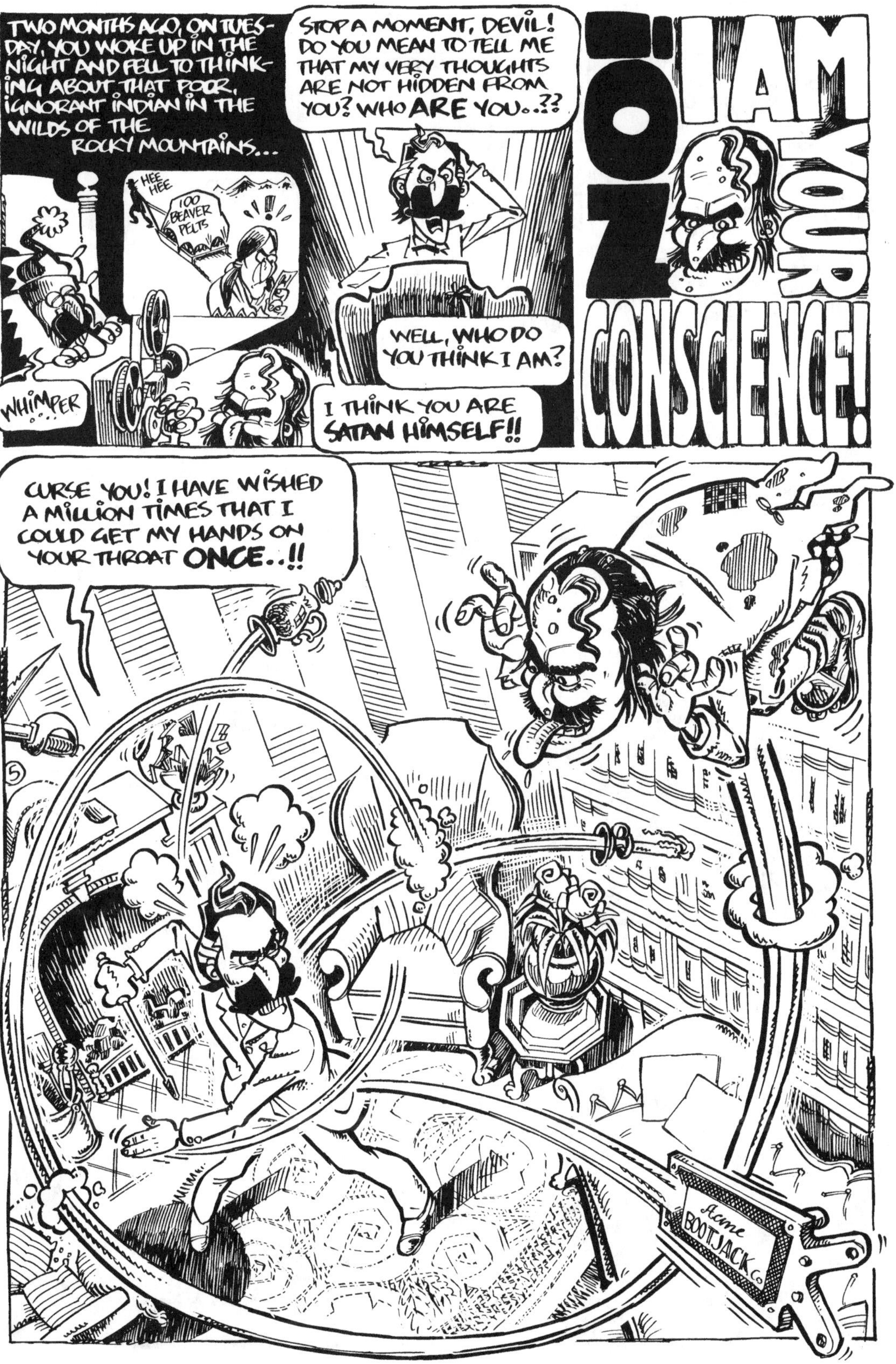
TWO MONTHS AGO, ON TUESDAY, YOU WOKE UP IN THE NIGHT AND FELL TO THINKING ABOUT THAT POOR, IGNORANT INDIAN IN THE WILDS OF THE ROCKY MOUNTAINS...
HEE HEE
100 BEAVER PELTS
WHIMPER
STOP A MOMENT, DEVIL! DO YOU MEAN TO TELL ME THAT MY VERY THOUGHTS ARE NOT HIDDEN FROM YOU? WHO ARE YOU..??
WELL, WHO DO YOU THINK I AM?
I THINK YOU ARE SATAN HIMSELF!!
"NO" I AM YOUR CONSCIENCE!
CURSE YOU! I HAVE WISHED A MILLION TIMES THAT I COULD GET MY HANDS ON YOUR THROAT ONCE..!!
Acme BOOTJACK Co.

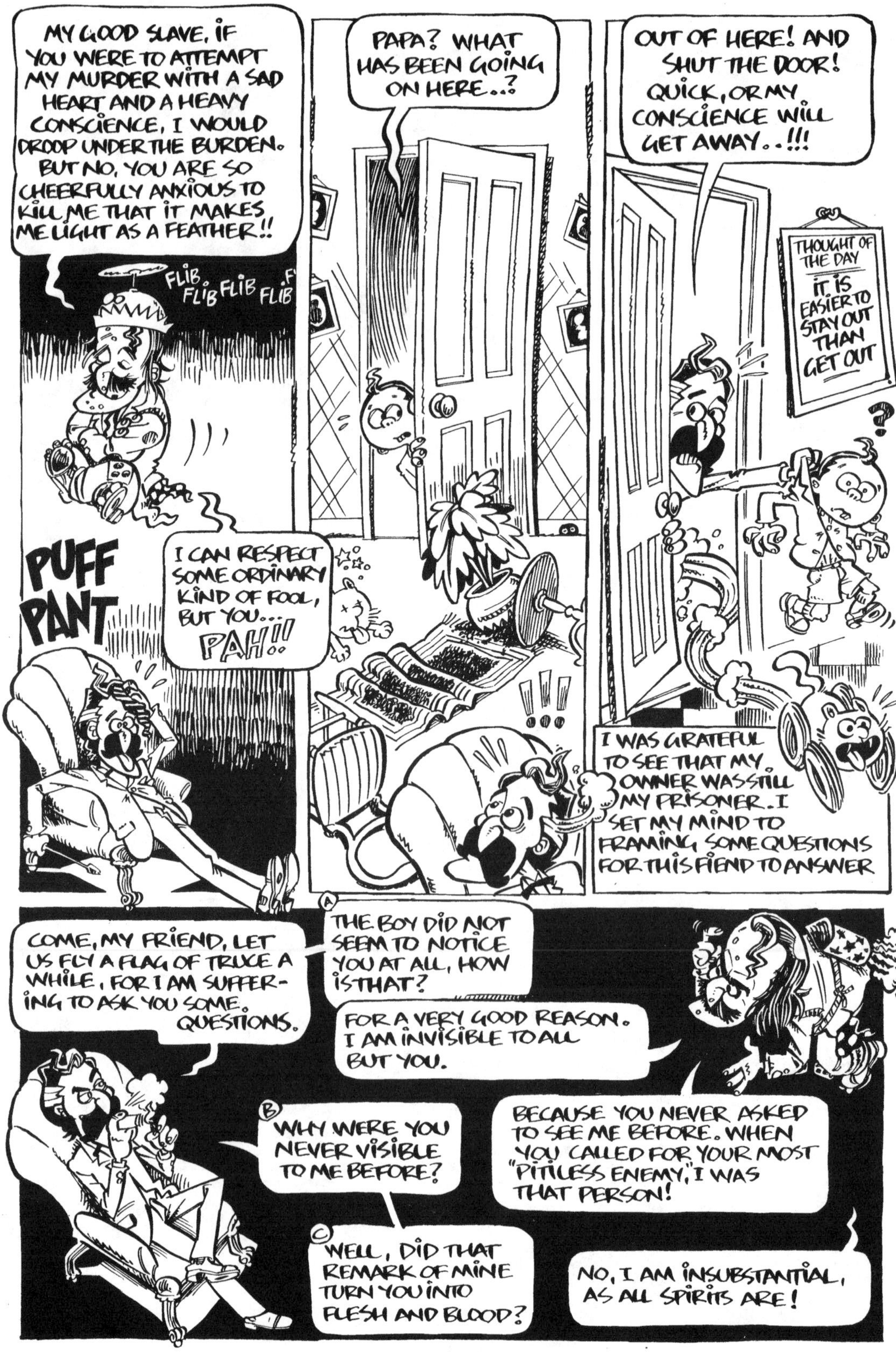
MY GOOD SLAVE, IF YOU WERE TO ATTEMPT MY MURDER WITH A SAD HEART AND A HEAVY CONSCIENCE, I WOULD DROOP UNDER THE BURDEN. BUT NO, YOU ARE SO CHEERFULLY ANXIOUS TO KILL ME THAT IT MAKES ME LIGHT AS A FEATHER!!
FLIB FLIB FLIB FLIB
PUFF
PANT
I CAN RESPECT SOME ORDINARY KIND OF FOOL, BUT YOU... PAH!!
PAPA? WHAT HAS BEEN GOING ON HERE..?
OUT OF HERE! AND SHUT THE DOOR! QUICK, OR MY CONSCIENCE WILL GET AWAY..!!!
THOUGHT OF THE DAY
IT IS EASIER TO STAY OUT THAN GET OUT
I WAS GRATEFUL TO SEE THAT MY OWNER WAS STILL MY PRISONER. I SET MY MIND TO FRAMING SOME QUESTIONS FOR THIS FIEND TO ANSWER
COME, MY FRIEND, LET US FLY A FLAG OF TRUCE A WHILE, FOR I AM SUFFERING TO ASK YOU SOME QUESTIONS.
A
THE BOY DID NOT SEEM TO NOTICE YOU AT ALL, HOW IS THAT?
FOR A VERY GOOD REASON. I AM INVISIBLE TO ALL BUT YOU.
B
WHY WERE YOU NEVER VISIBLE TO ME BEFORE?
BECAUSE YOU NEVER ASKED TO SEE ME BEFORE. WHEN YOU CALLED FOR YOUR MOST "PITILESS ENEMY," I WAS THAT PERSON!
C
WELL, DID THAT REMARK OF MINE TURN YOU INTO FLESH AND BLOOD?
NO, I AM INSUBSTANTIAL, AS ALL SPIRITS ARE!

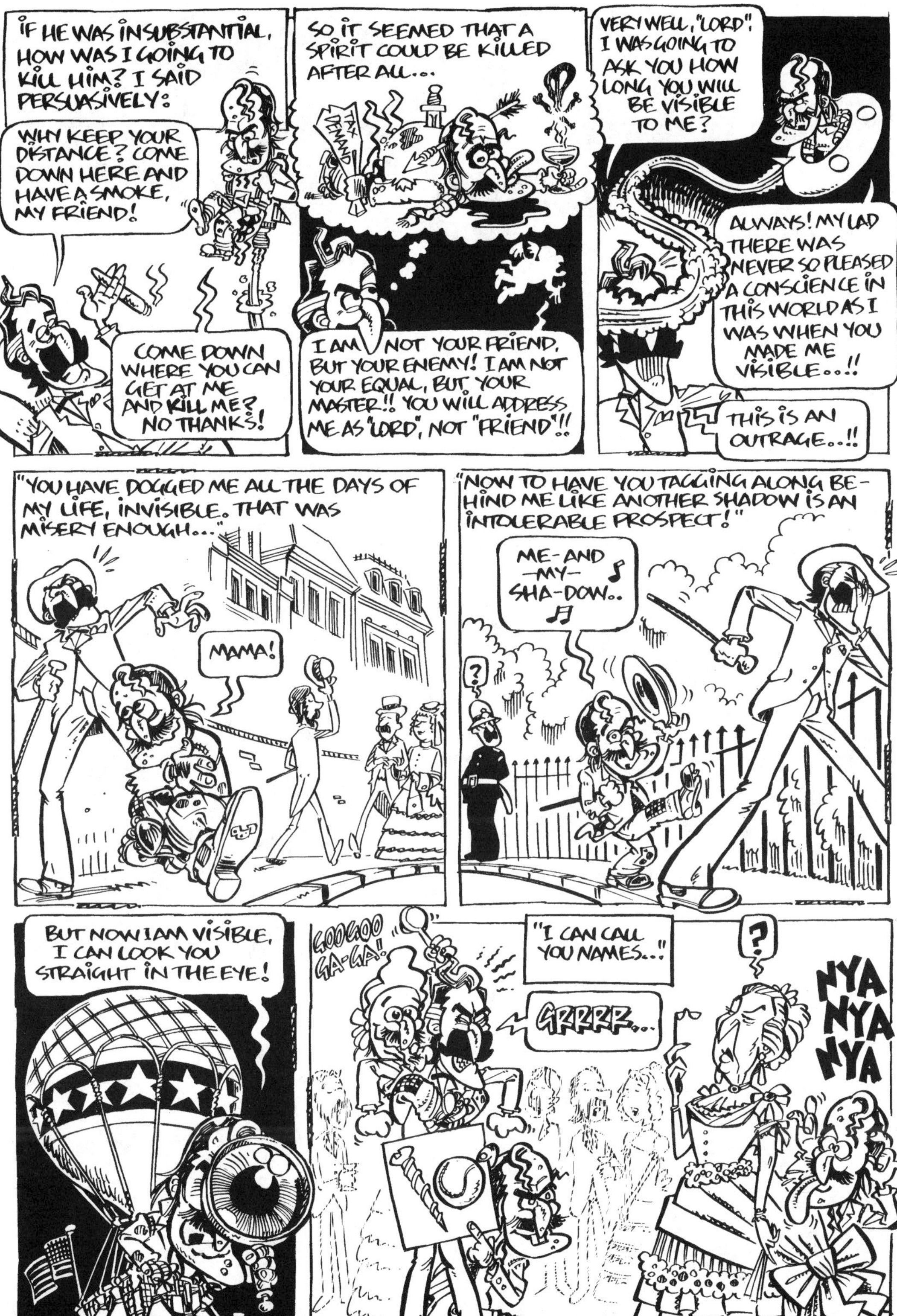
IF HE WAS INSUBSTANTIAL, HOW WAS I GOING TO KILL HIM? I SAID PERSUASIVELY:
WHY KEEP YOUR DISTANCE? COME DOWN HERE AND HAVE A SMOKE, MY FRIEND!
COME DOWN WHERE YOU CAN GET AT ME AND KILL ME? NO THANKS!
SO IT SEEMED THAT A SPIRIT COULD BE KILLED AFTER ALL...
TAX DEMAND
I AM NOT YOUR FRIEND, BUT YOUR ENEMY! I AM NOT YOUR EQUAL, BUT, YOUR MASTER!! YOU WILL ADDRESS ME AS "LORD", NOT "FRIEND"!!
VERY WELL, "LORD", I WAS GOING TO ASK YOU HOW LONG YOU WILL BE VISIBLE TO ME?
ALWAYS! MY LAD THERE WAS NEVER SO PLEASED A CONSCIENCE IN THIS WORLD AS I WAS WHEN YOU MADE ME VISIBLE...!!
THIS IS AN OUTRAGE...!!
"YOU HAVE DOGGED ME ALL THE DAYS OF MY LIFE, INVISIBLE. THAT WAS MISERY ENOUGH..."
MAMA!
"NOW TO HAVE YOU TAGGING ALONG BEHIND ME LIKE ANOTHER SHADOW IS AN INTOLERABLE PROSPECT!"
ME-AND -MY- SHA-DOW..
?
BUT NOW I AM VISIBLE, I CAN LOOK YOU STRAIGHT IN THE EYE!
GOOGOO GA-GA!
"I CAN CALL YOU NAMES...!"
GRRRR...
?
NYA NYA NYA NYA

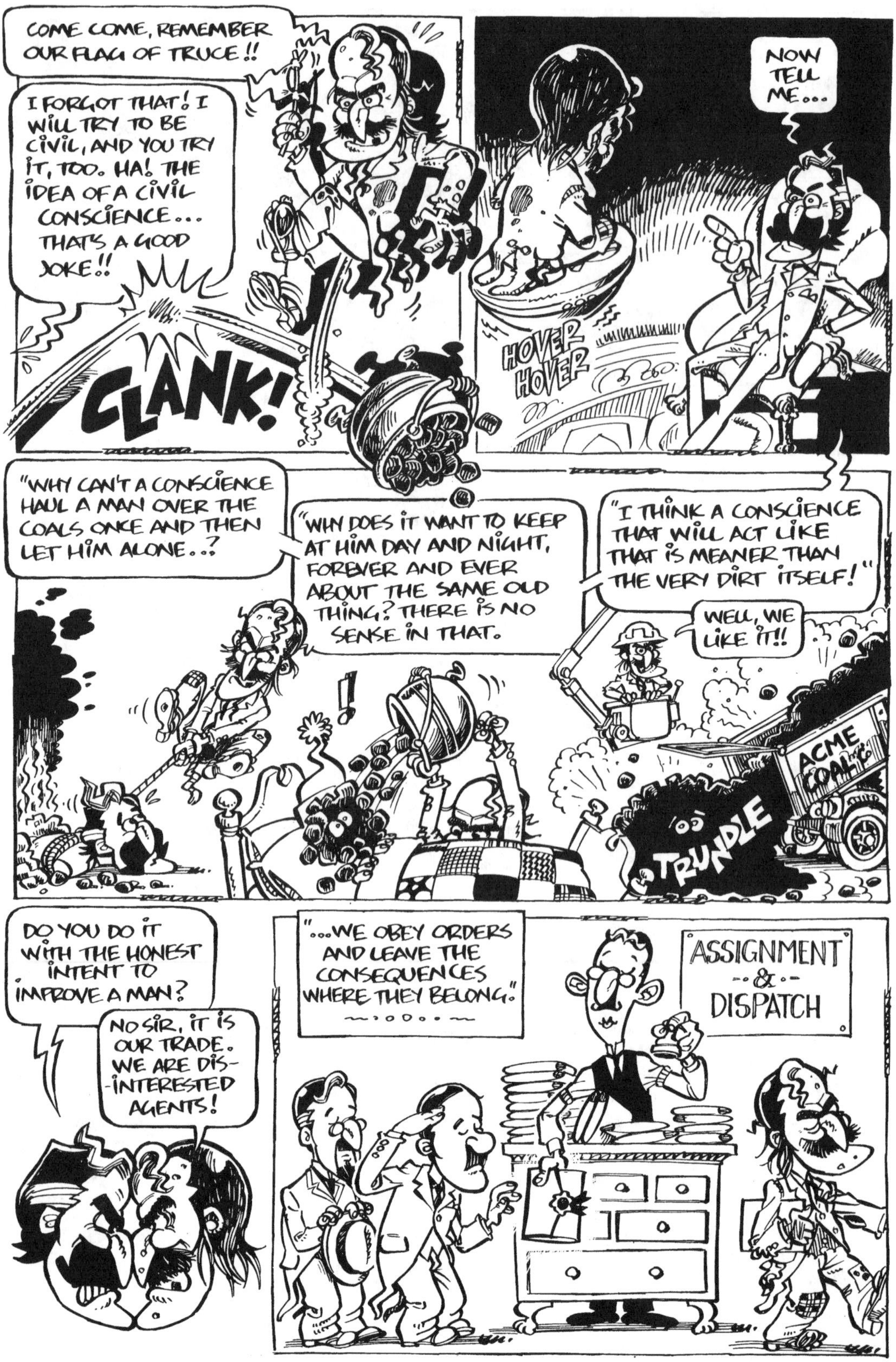
COME COME, REMEMBER OUR FLAG OF TRUCE!!
I FORGOT THAT! I WILL TRY TO BE CIVIL, AND YOU TRY IT, TOO. HA! THE IDEA OF A CIVIL CONSCIENCE... THAT'S A GOOD JOKE!!
CLANK!
NOW TELL ME...
HOVER HOVER
"WHY CAN'T A CONSCIENCE HAUL A MAN OVER THE COALS ONCE AND THEN LET HIM ALONE..?
"WHY DOES IT WANT TO KEEP AT HIM DAY AND NIGHT, FOREVER AND EVER ABOUT THE SAME OLD THING? THERE IS NO SENSE IN THAT.
"I THINK A CONSCIENCE THAT WILL ACT LIKE THAT IS MEANER THAN THE VERY DIRT ITSELF!"
WELL, WE LIKE IT!!
ACME COAL Co.
TRUNDLE
DO YOU DO IT WITH THE HONEST INTENT TO IMPROVE A MAN?
NO SIR, IT IS OUR TRADE. WE ARE DIS-INTERESTED AGENTS!
"...WE OBEY ORDERS AND LEAVE THE CONSEQUENCES WHERE THEY BELONG."
ASSIGNMENT & DISPATCH

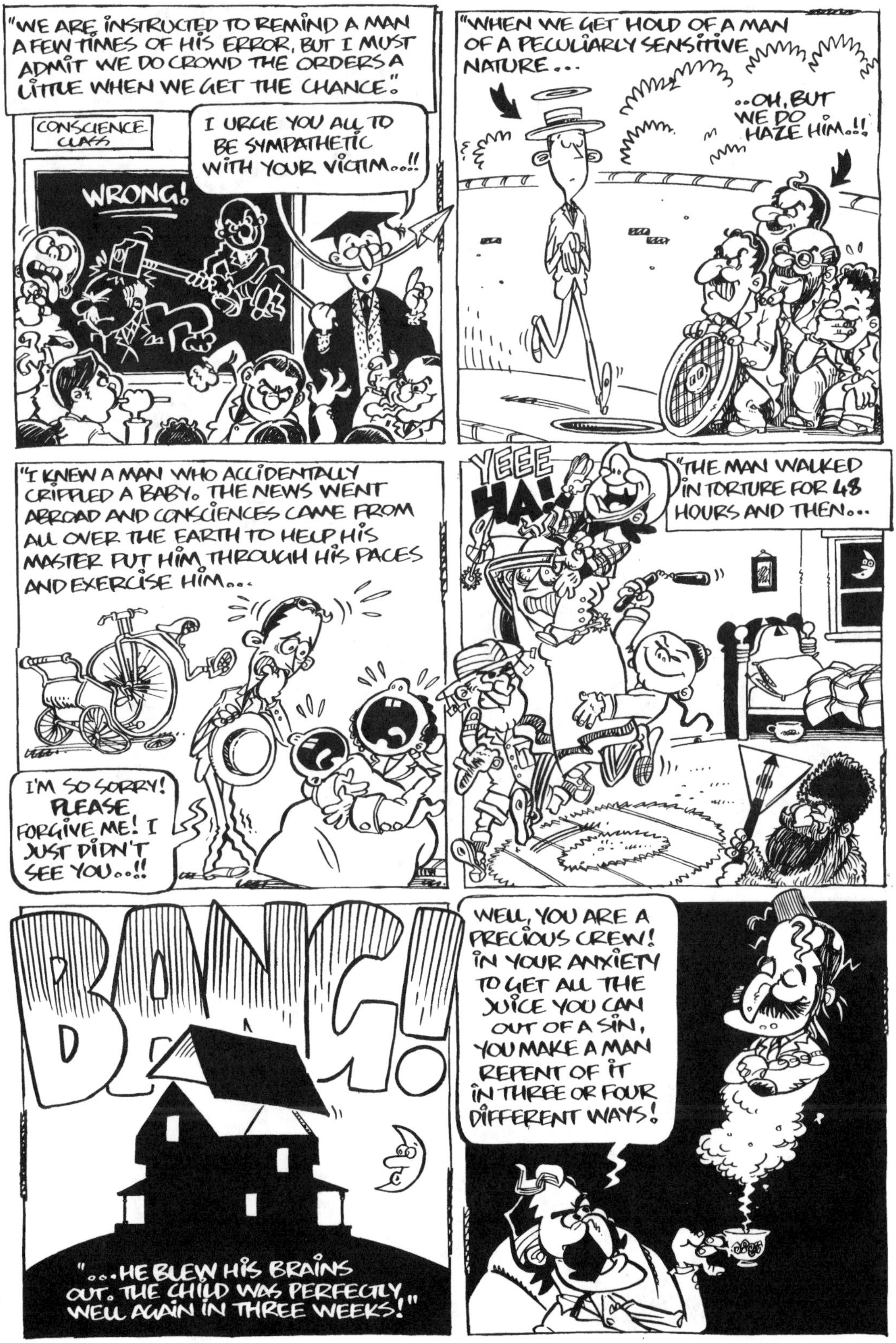
"WE ARE INSTRUCTED TO REMIND A MAN A FEW TIMES OF HIS ERROR, BUT I MUST ADMIT WE DO CROWD THE ORDERS A LITTLE WHEN WE GET THE CHANCE."
CONSCIENCE CLASS
I URGE YOU ALL TO BE SYMPATHETIC WITH YOUR VICTIM...!!
WRONG!
"WHEN WE GET HOLD OF A MAN OF A PECULIARLY SENSITIVE NATURE...
..OH, BUT WE DO HAZE HIM..!!
"I KNEW A MAN WHO ACCIDENTALLY CRIPPLED A BABY. THE NEWS WENT ABROAD AND CONSCIENCES CAME FROM ALL OVER THE EARTH TO HELP HIS MASTER PUT HIM THROUGH HIS PACES AND EXERCISE HIM...
I'M SO SORRY! PLEASE FORGIVE ME! I JUST DIDN'T SEE YOU..!!
YEEE HA!
"THE MAN WALKED IN TORTURE FOR 48 HOURS AND THEN...
BANG!
"...HE BLEW HIS BRAINS OUT. THE CHILD WAS PERFECTLY WELL AGAIN IN THREE WEEKS!"
WELL, YOU ARE A PRECIOUS CREW! IN YOUR ANXIETY TO GET ALL THE JUICE YOU CAN OUT OF A SIN, YOU MAKE A MAN REPENT OF IT IN THREE OR FOUR DIFFERENT WAYS!

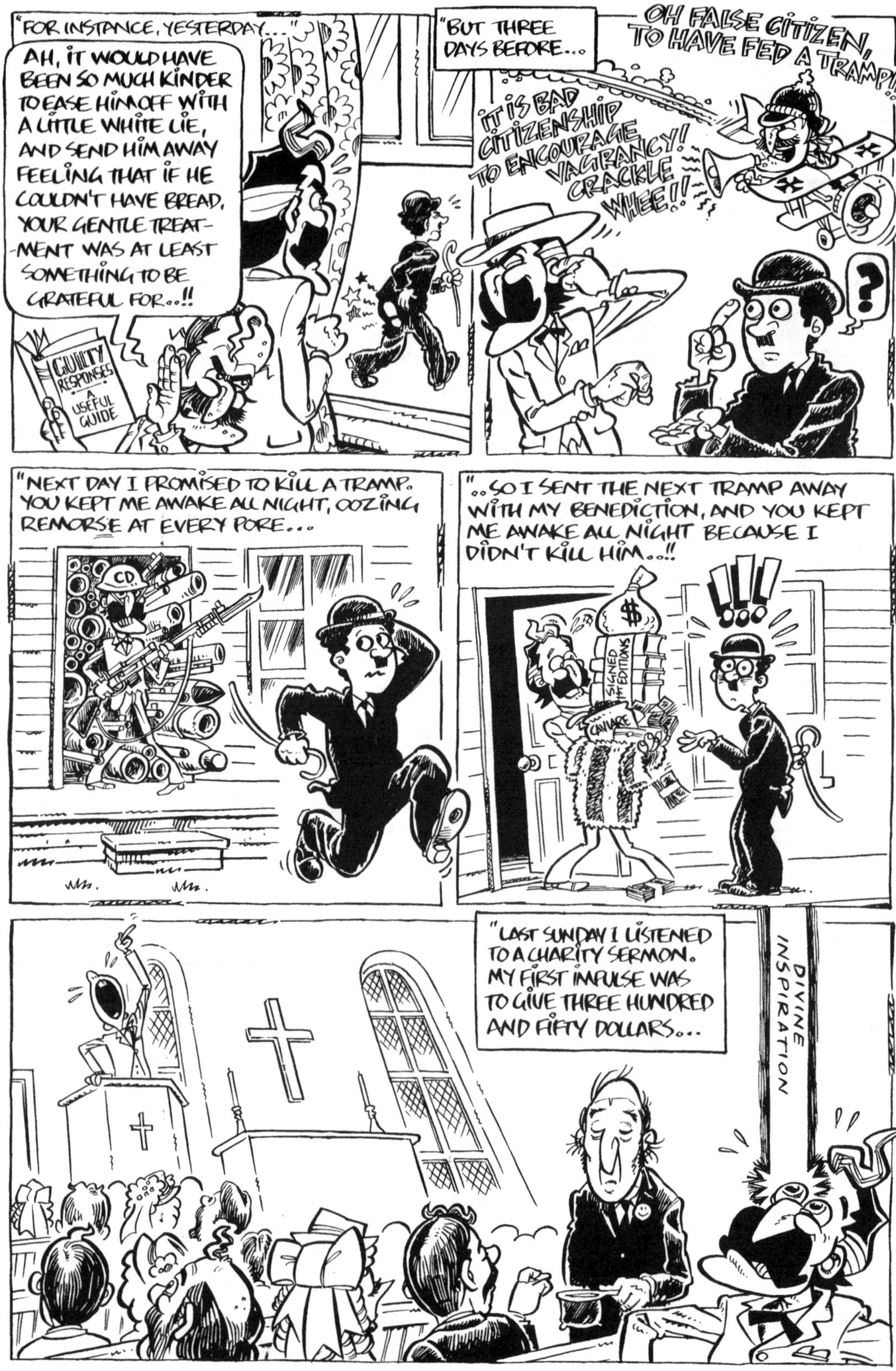
"FOR INSTANCE, YESTERDAY..."
AH, IT WOULD HAVE BEEN SO MUCH KINDER TO EASE HIM OFF WITH A LITTLE WHITE LIE, AND SEND HIM AWAY FEELING THAT IF HE COULDN'T HAVE BREAD, YOUR GENTLE TREAT-MENT WAS AT LEAST SOMETHING TO BE GRATEFUL FOR..!!
GUILTY RESPONSES A USEFUL GUIDE
"BUT THREE DAYS BEFORE..."
OH FALSE CITIZEN, TO HAVE FED A TRAMP!!
IT IS BAD CITIZENSHIP TO ENCOURAGE VAGRANCY! VAGRANCY CRACKLE WHEE!!
?
"NEXT DAY I PROMISED TO KILL A TRAMP. YOU KEPT ME AWAKE ALL NIGHT, OOZING REMORSE AT EVERY PORE...
CD
"..SO I SENT THE NEXT TRAMP AWAY WITH MY BENEDICTION, AND YOU KEPT ME AWAKE ALL NIGHT BECAUSE I DIDN'T KILL HIM..!!
$
SIGNED 1st EDITIONS
CAVIARE
!!!
"LAST SUNDAY I LISTENED TO A CHARITY SERMON. MY FIRST IMPULSE WAS TO GIVE THREE HUNDRED AND FIFTY DOLLARS...
DIVINE INSPIRATION

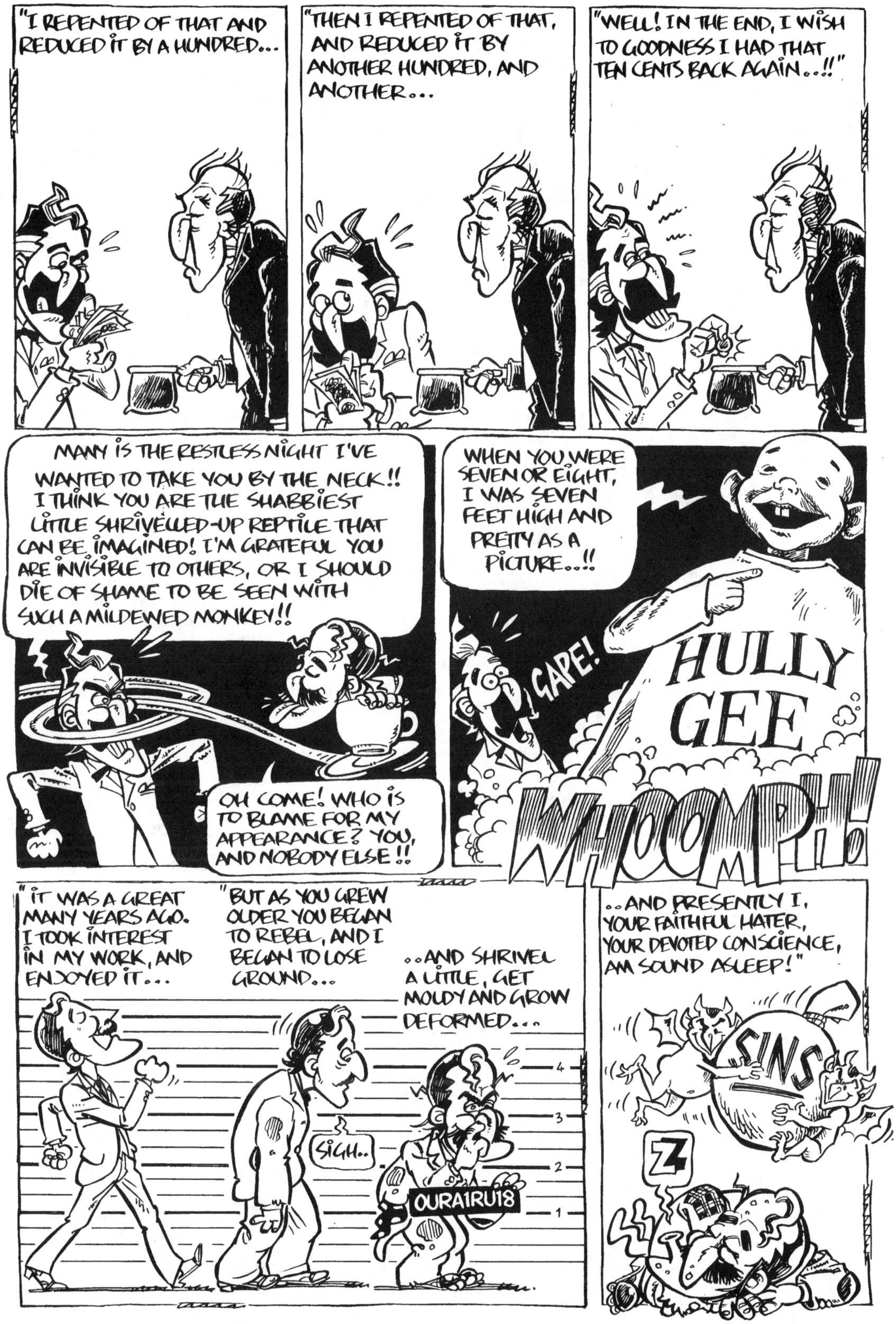
"I REPENTED OF THAT AND REDUCED IT BY A HUNDRED...
"THEN I REPENTED OF THAT, AND REDUCED IT BY ANOTHER HUNDRED, AND ANOTHER...
"WELL! IN THE END, I WISH TO GOODNESS I HAD THAT TEN CENTS BACK AGAIN..!!"
MANY IS THE RESTLESS NIGHT I'VE WANTED TO TAKE YOU BY THE NECK!! I THINK YOU ARE THE SHABBIEST LITTLE SHRIVELLED-UP REPTILE THAT CAN BE IMAGINED! I'M GRATEFUL YOU ARE INVISIBLE TO OTHERS, OR I SHOULD DIE OF SHAME TO BE SEEN WITH SUCH A MILDEWED MONKEY!!
OH COME! WHO IS TO BLAME FOR MY APPEARANCE? YOU, AND NOBODY ELSE!!
WHEN YOU WERE SEVEN OR EIGHT, I WAS SEVEN FEET HIGH AND PRETTY AS A PICTURE..!!
GAPE!
HULLY GEE
WHOOMPH!
"IT WAS A GREAT MANY YEARS AGO. I TOOK INTEREST IN MY WORK, AND ENJOYED IT...
"BUT AS YOU GREW OLDER YOU BEGAN TO REBEL, AND I BEGAN TO LOSE GROUND...
..AND SHRIVEL A LITTLE, GET MOLDY AND GROW DEFORMED...
SIGH..
4
3
2
1
OURA1RU18
..AND PRESENTLY I, YOUR FAITHFUL HATER, YOUR DEVOTED CONSCIENCE, AM SOUND ASLEEP!"
SINS
Z

I WISH I HAD KNOWN THIS SOME THIRTY YEARS AGO – I SHOULD HAVE TURNED MY PARTICULAR ATTENTION TO SIN! BY THIS TIME I SHOULD NOT ONLY HAVE HAD YOU PERMANENTLY ASLEEP...

"... BUT REDUCED TO THE SIZE OF A HOMEOPATHIC PILL! I WOULD FEED YOU TO A YELLOW DOG..!!"

FIDO! HERE BOY! I HAVE SOMETHING FOR YOU..!

HELP ME! HELLPP! MEEEE..!

YIP!

DO YOU KNOW A GOOD MANY CONSCIENCES?

PLENTY OF THEM!

COULD YOU BRING THEM HERE?

NO!

WOULD THEY BE VISIBLE TO ME?

NO!

TELL ME ABOUT MY NEIGHBOUR THOMPSON'S CONSCIENCE!

I KNEW HIM WHEN HE WAS ELEVEN FEET HIGH!

..AS TO HIS PRESENT SIZE, ..WELL, HE SLEEPS IN A CIGAR BOX!!

DO YOU KNOW ROBINSON'S CONSCIENCE?

YES, HE IS SHAPELY AND COMELY..!!

DO YOU KNOW TOM SMITH'S CONSCIENCE?

HE IS THIRTY-SEVEN FEET HIGH AND NEVER SLEEPS. HE IS THE PRESIDENT OF THE NEW ENGLAND CONSCIENCE CLUB. HE CAN MAKE POOR SMITH IMAGINE THAT THE MOST INNOCENT LITTLE THING HE DOES IS AN ODIOUS SIN!

SMITH IS THE NOBLEST AND PUREST MAN. ONLY A CONSCIENCE COULD FIND PLEASURE IN HEAPING AGONY UPON A SPIRIT LIKE THAT..!

YOU KNOW MY AUNT MARY'S CONSCIENCE?

I HAVE SEEN HER AT A DISTANCE. SHE LIVES IN THE OPEN AIR, BE-CAUSE NO DOOR IS LARGE ENOUGH TO ADMIT HER !!

I CAN BELIEVE THAT! DO YOU KNOW THE CONSCIENCE OF THAT PUBLISHER WHO STOLE SOME SKETCHES OF MINE?

THE TINIEST CON-SCIENCE IN THE WORLD!!

YES, HE HAS A WIDE FAME. HE WAS EXHIBITED AT A SHOW A MONTH AGO. THE MANAGE-MENT COULD ONLY PROVIDE A MICRO-SCOPE WITH A MAGNIFYING POWER OF THIRTY THOUSAND DIAMETERS, SO NO-BODY GOT TO SEE HIM! THERE WAS GENERAL DISSATISFACTION!!

86

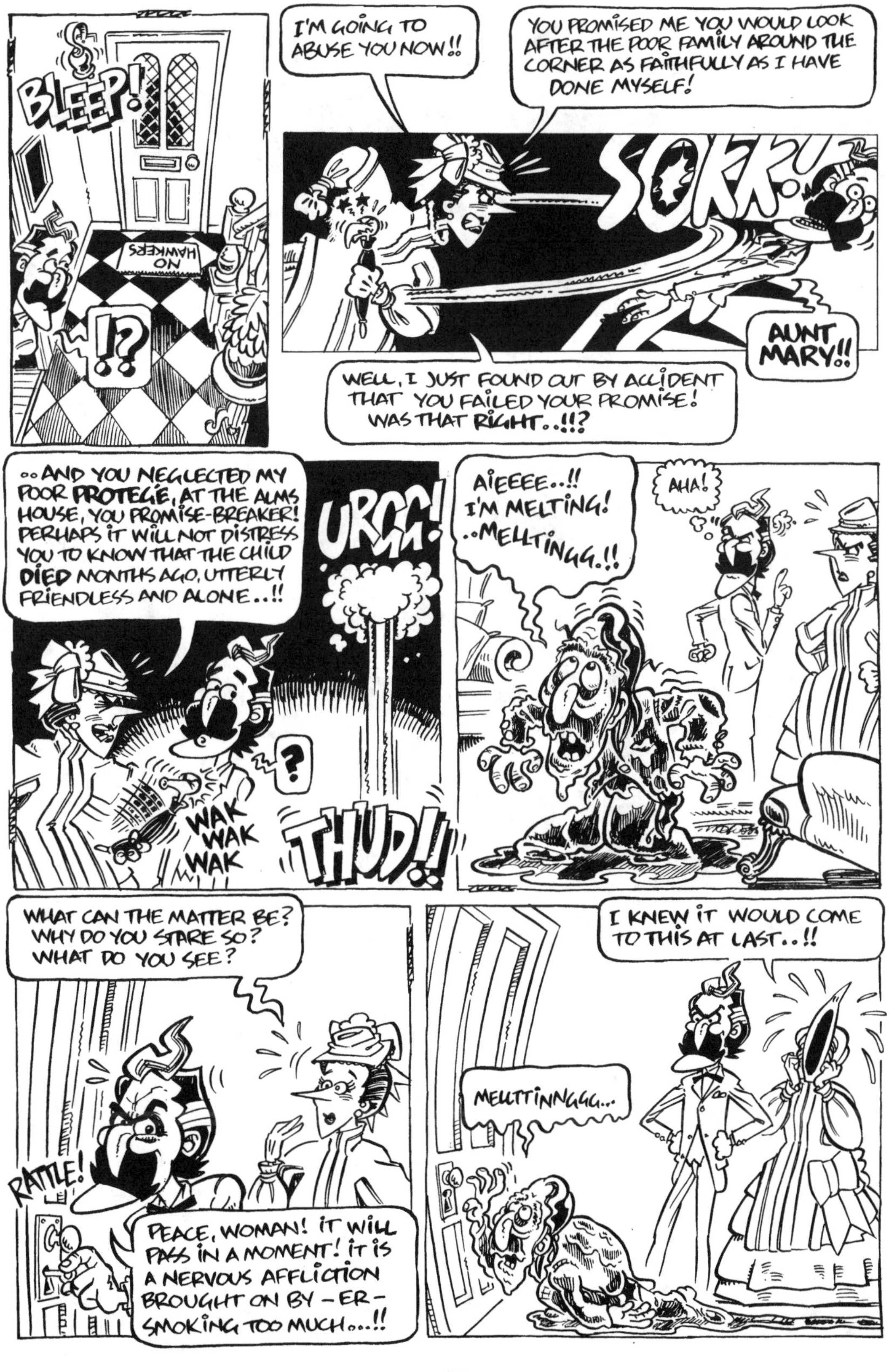
BLEEP!
NO HAWKERS
!?
I'M GOING TO ABUSE YOU NOW!!
YOU PROMISED ME YOU WOULD LOOK AFTER THE POOR FAMILY AROUND THE CORNER AS FAITHFULLY AS I HAVE DONE MYSELF!
SOKK!
AUNT MARY!!
WELL, I JUST FOUND OUT BY ACCIDENT THAT YOU FAILED YOUR PROMISE! WAS THAT RIGHT..!!?
..AND YOU NEGLECTED MY POOR PROTEGÉ, AT THE ALMS HOUSE, YOU PROMISE-BREAKER! PERHAPS IT WILL NOT DISTRESS YOU TO KNOW THAT THE CHILD DIED MONTHS AGO, UTTERLY FRIENDLESS AND ALONE..!!
URGG!
?
WAK WAK WAK
THUD!!
AIEEEE..!! I'M MELTING! ..MELLTINGG.!!
AHA!
WHAT CAN THE MATTER BE? WHY DO YOU STARE SO? WHAT DO YOU SEE?
RATTLE!
PEACE, WOMAN! IT WILL PASS IN A MOMENT! IT IS A NERVOUS AFFLICTION BROUGHT ON BY -ER- SMOKING TOO MUCH...!!
I KNEW IT WOULD COME TO THIS AT LAST..!!
MELLTINNGGG...

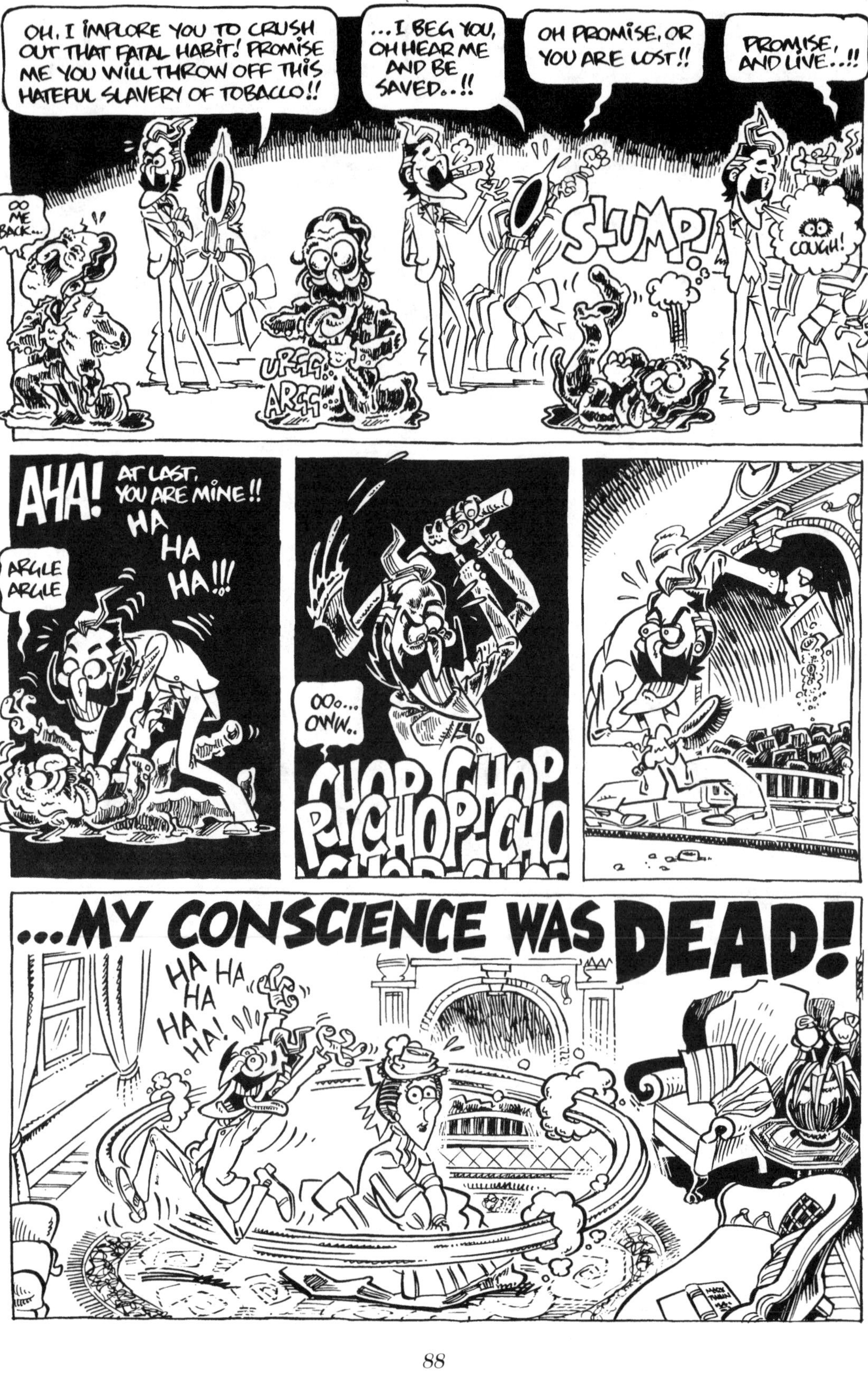
OH, I IMPLORE YOU TO CRUSH OUT THAT FATAL HABIT! PROMISE ME YOU WILL THROW OFF THIS HATEFUL SLAVERY OF TOBACCO!!
...I BEG YOU, OH HEAR ME AND BE SAVED..!!
OH PROMISE, OR YOU ARE LOST!!
PROMISE, AND LIVE..!!
OO ME BACK...
URGG.. ARGG..
SLUMP!
COUGH!
AHA!
AT LAST, YOU ARE MINE!!
HA HA HA!!!
ARGLE ARGLE
OO... OWW..
CHOP CHOP
CHOP-CHO
...MY CONSCIENCE WAS DEAD!
HA HA HA HA HA!

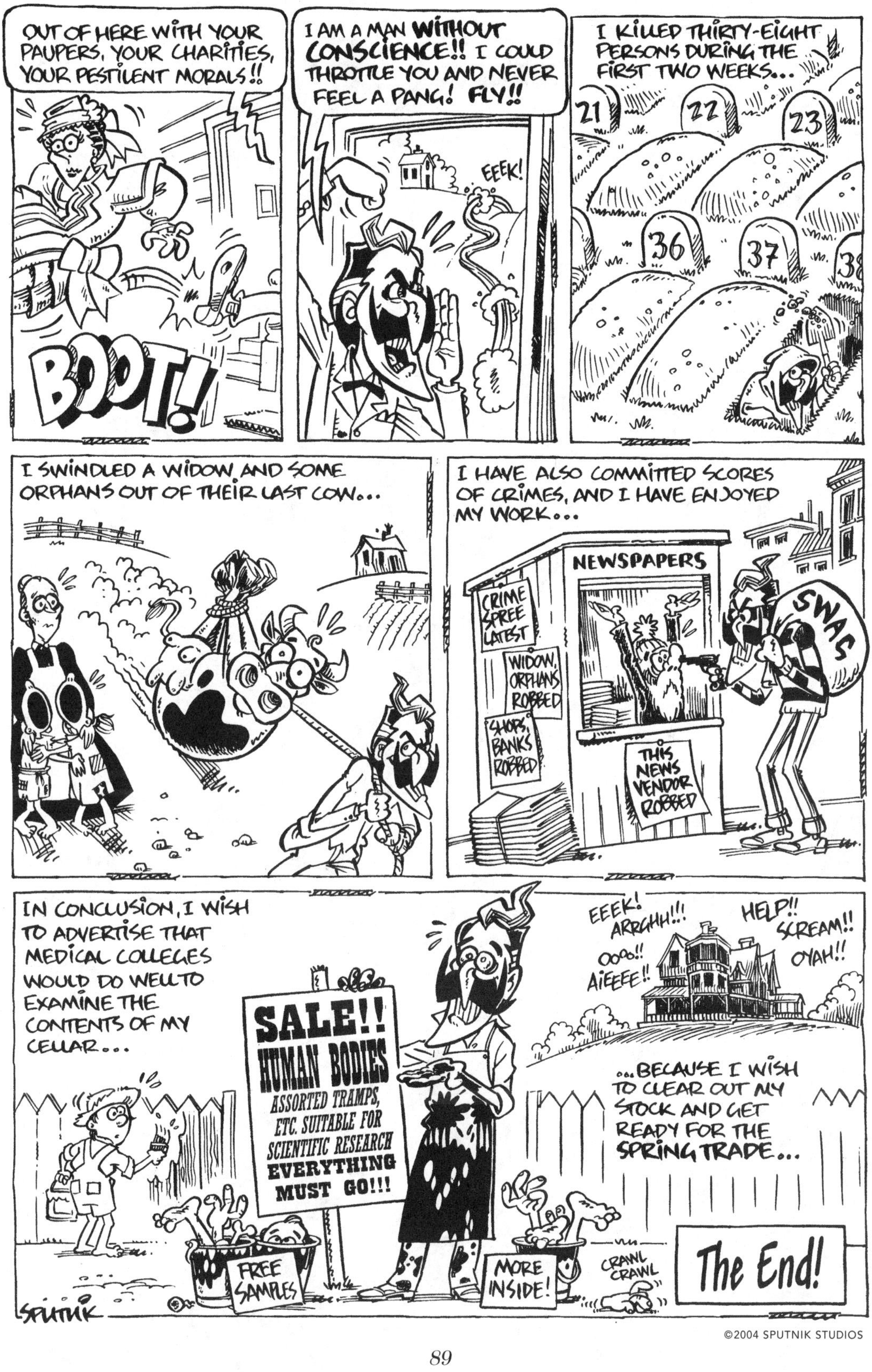
OUT OF HERE WITH YOUR PAUPERS, YOUR CHARITIES, YOUR PESTILENT MORALS!!
BOOT!
I AM A MAN WITHOUT CONSCIENCE!! I COULD THROTTLE YOU AND NEVER FEEL A PANG! FLY!!
EEEK!
I KILLED THIRTY-EIGHT PERSONS DURING THE FIRST TWO WEEKS...
21
22
23
36
37
I SWINDLED A WIDOW AND SOME ORPHANS OUT OF THEIR LAST COW...
I HAVE ALSO COMMITTED SCORES OF CRIMES, AND I HAVE ENJOYED MY WORK...
NEWSPAPERS
CRIME SPREE LATEST
WIDOW, ORPHANS ROBBED
SHOPS, BANKS ROBBED
THIS NEWS VENDOR ROBBED
SWAG
IN CONCLUSION, I WISH TO ADVERTISE THAT MEDICAL COLLEGES WOULD DO WELL TO EXAMINE THE CONTENTS OF MY CELLAR...
SALE!! HUMAN BODIES ASSORTED TRAMPS, ETC. SUITABLE FOR SCIENTIFIC RESEARCH EVERYTHING MUST GO!!!
EEEK! ARRGHH!!! HELP!! SCREAM!! OOOO!! AIEEEE!! OYAH!!
...BECAUSE I WISH TO CLEAR OUT MY STOCK AND GET READY FOR THE SPRING TRADE...
FREE SAMPLES
MORE INSIDE!
CRAWL CRAWL
The End!
SPUTNIK

A CURIOUS PLEASURE EXCURSION

Being a Public Service Announcement by **Mark Twain**

THIS IS TO INFORM **THE PUBLIC** *that as of* **JUNE 1, 1874**

in connection with **MR. P. T. BARNUM** *I have leased the* **CELESTIAL BODY**

Known as **COGGIA'S COMET**

and

I DESIRE to solicit the **PUBLIC PATRONAGE** in favor of a **BENEFICIAL ENTERPRISE** *which we have in view.*

Illustrated by **William L. Brown**

WE PROPOSE

To FIT UP

COMFORTABLE, And

Even LUXURIOUS,

ACCOMMODATIONS In The

TAIL OF THE COMET

FOR As Many PERSONS

As Will HONOR Us *WITH* Their PATRONAGE,

And MAKE AN EXTENDED EXCURSION AMONG

THE HEAVENLY BODIES.

The *COMET* Will Leave *NEW YORK*

At 10 P.M. On The 20TH OF JUNE,

and *THEREFORE* it will be DESIRABLE

That The PASSENGERS Be *ON BOARD*

BY EIGHT AT THE LATEST

To Avoid Confusion In Getting Under Way

NO DOGS WILL BE ALLOWED ON BOARD.

We Shall Have

BILLIARD ROOMS,

CARD Rooms,

MUSIC Rooms,

BOWLING ALLEYS

and Spacious THEATERS

and LIBRARIES;

And On The MAIN DECK We Propose To Have

A DRIVING PARK,

With Upward Of

100,000 MILES OF ROADWAY.

Meals Served In Staterooms Charged Extra.

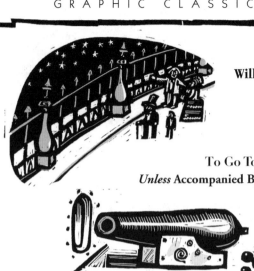

The SAFETY of the Passengers
Will *IN ALL WAYS* Be Jealously Looked To.
A SUBSTANTIAL IRON RAILING
Will Be Put Up
All Around The Comet,
And NO ONE Will Be Allowed
To Go To The EDGE And Look Over
Unless Accompanied By Either My *Partner* Or *Myself.*

Hostility Is Not Apprehended
From Any INHABITANTS OF THE STARS,
But We Have Thought It Best To Err On The SAFE Side,
And *Therefore* Have Provided Sufficient
ARMAMENTS, Including *A Proper Number* Of
MORTARS, SIEGE GUNS, *And* BOARDING PIKES.

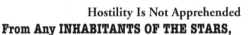

We Shall Hope To leave a
GOOD IMPRESSION OF AMERICA
Behind Us *But* **At The Same Time**
We Shall PROMPTLY *Resent* Any *Injury*
That May Be Done Us *Or* Any *Insolence* Offered Us,
By *PARTIES* or *GOVERNMENTS*
Residing In ANY STAR *In The Firmament.*

We Shall Take With Us A GREAT FORCE
Of MISSIONARIES, And *Shed The True Light*
Upon The CELESTIAL ORBS Which,
Physically Aglow, Are Yet Morally In Darkness.
SUNDAY SCHOOLS And COMPULSORY EDUCATION
Will Be Established *Wherever Practicable.*

The *Comet* Will Visit *MARS* first,
And proceed to
MERCURY, JUPITER,
VENUS, and SATURN.
Every STAR of *Prominent Magnitude*,
And Every Constellation Of Importance
Will Be Visited, With Time Allowed For
EXCURSIONS To *Points Of Interest* Inland.

First-Class Fare Will Be Charged
At *The Low Rate* Of $2
For *Every* **50,000,000 Miles Of** *Actual Travel.*
Passengers Desiring To Diverge
AT ANY POINT
Will Be Transferred To Other Comets.
We *Will* Make *Connections*
AT PRINCIPAL POINTS
With All Reliable Lines.

Passengers Paying **Double Fare**
Will Be *Entitled* To A Share
In All The New
Stars, Suns, Moons, And Meteors
We May Discover.
Advertisers Will Take Notice
That We Will Carry *Billboards* Along
For **Use** In The **Constellations**,
And Are Open To Terms.

For Further Particulars, Apply On Board, Or To My Partner, But Not To Me, Since I Do Not Take Charge Of The Comet Until She Is Under Way. It Is Necessary, At A Time Like This, That My Mind Should Not Be Burdened With Small Business Details.

-Mark Twain

Is He Living or Is He Dead?

a story by Mark Twain

illustrated by Simon Gane

I was spending the month of March 1892 in Menton, on the Riviera. At this retired spot one has all the advantages which are to be had at Monte Carlo and Nice, without the fuss and feathers. Menton is quiet, unpretentious; now and then a rich man comes, and I presently got acquainted with one of these. I will call him Smith.

One day, at breakfast, he exclaimed:

Quick! Cast your eye on the man going out at the door.

Why? Do you know who he is?

Yes. He spent several days here before you came. He is a retired, and very rich, silk manufacturer from Lyon, they say, and I guess he is alone in the world, for he always looks sad and dreamy, and doesn't talk with anybody. His name is Theophile Magnan.

I supposed that Smith would now proceed to justify the large interest which he had shown in Monsieur Magnan, but, instead, he began to tell one of Hans Andersen's little stories:

"A child has a caged bird which it loves but thoughtlessly neglects. The bird pours out its song unheard and unheeded; but in time, hunger and thirst assail the creature, and finally, it dies.

"The child comes, is smitten with remorse, and buries the bird with elaborate pomp and the tenderest grief, without knowing that it isn't children only who starve poets to death and then spend enough on their funerals and monuments to have kept them alive and made them easy and comfortable."

I will now tell you a curious history. It has been a secret for many years - a secret between me and three others; but I am going to break the seal.

A long time ago I was a young artist. I wandered about France, sketching, and was presently joined by a couple of young Frenchmen who were doing much the same thing.

"Claude Frère

"and Carl Boulanger...

"dear fellows, and the sunniest souls who ever laughed at poverty.

"At last, an artist as poor as ourselves took us in and literally saved us from starving—

"François Millet."

What! The great François Millet?

"He wasn't any greater than we were, then. He was so poor that he had nothing to feed us on but turnips. We four became fast friends. We painted together, piling up stock, but very seldom getting rid of any of it. We had lovely times together; but how we were pinched!

"For a little over two years this went on. At last, one day, Claude said:

Boys, we've come to the end. I've been all around the village and they all refuse to credit us for another centime until all the debts are paid up.

we realized that our circumstances were desperate now. Carl said:

It's a shame! Look at these canvases: stacks of pictures as good as anybody in Europe paints - and plenty of strangers have said the same.

But didn't buy.

No matter, they said it; and it's true. Look at your ANGELUS there!

Pah! I was offered five francs for it.

Why didn't you take it?

I thought he would give more—so I asked him eight.

Well—and then?

He said he would call again.

Why, François—

Oh, I know! It was a mistake, and I was a fool.

Well don't be a fool again.

I wish somebody would come along and offer us a cabbage for it—You'd see!

A cabbage! Oh, don't name it—it makes my mouth water.

"'Boys,' said Carl, 'do these pictures lack merit? Answer me that!'"

NO!

If an illustrious name were attached to them they would sell at splendid prices. Isn't that so?

Certainly it is. How does that concern us?

In this way, comrades—we'll attach an illustrious name to them!

"The conversation stopped. The faces turned inquiringly upon Carl. He sat down, and said:

Now, I have a perfectly serious thing to propose. I think it is the only way to keep us out of the almshouse, and I believe my project will make us all rich.

Rich! You've lost your mind.

NO, I haven't.

Carl, you want to take a pill and get right to bed.

Bandage him first - bandage his head and then—

Shut up!

Let the boy have his say. Now then—come out with your project, Carl. What is it?

Well, I will ask you to note this fact in human history: that the merit of many a great artist has never been acknowledged until after he was starved and dead. Then his pictures climb to high prices after his death. My project is this: we must cast lots—one of us must die.

"There was a wild chorus of advice for the help of Carl's brain; but he waited for the hilarity to calm down, and then went on again:

Yes, one of us must die. We will cast lots. The one chosen shall be illustrious, all of us shall be rich.

During the next three months the one who is to die shall paint with all his might, enlarge his stock all he can - sketches, studies, fragments of studies, a dozen dabs of the brush on each - turn out fifty a day, each to contain some peculiarity or mannerism easily detectable as his - they're the things that are collected at fabulous prices after the great man is gone; we'll have a ton of them ready!

And all that time the rest of us will be working Paris and the dealers.

You get the idea?

But about this dying-

Don't you see? The man doesn't really die; he changes his name and vanishes; we bury a dummy and cry over it, with all the world to help.

"Everybody jumped up in joy and broke out into applause. For hours we talked over the great plan, and at last, when all the details had been arranged, we cast lots...

"...and Millet was elected to die.

"Next morning, we left a stake of turnips for Millet to live on for a few days and the three of us cleared out, on foot."

Each of us carried a dozen of Millet's small pictures, purposing to market them. Carl struck for Paris, where he would start the work of building up Millet's name against the coming great day. Claude and I were to separate, and scatter abroad over France.

"I walked two days before I began business. Then I began to sketch a villa in the outskirts of a big town – because I saw the proprietor standing on the veranda. He came down to look on, and said I was a master!

"I put down my brush, reached into my satchel, fetched out a Millet, and pointed to the cipher in the corner, I said proudly:

Well, he taught me! I should think I ought to know my trade!

"The man looked embarrassed, and I said sorrowfully:

You don't mean to intimate that you don't know the cipher of François Millet!

"Of course he didn't know that cipher; but he said:

Why, it is Millet's, sure enough! Of course I recognize it now.

Next, he wanted to buy it; and at last, I let him have it for eight hundred francs.

Eight hundred!

Yes. Millet would have sold it for a pork chop. I wish I could get it back for eighty thousand.

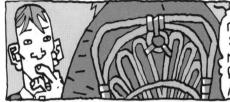

But that time's gone by. I made a very nice picture of that man's house and seeing as I was the pupil of such a master, I sold it to him for a hundred francs. I sent the eight hundred to Millet and struck out again next day.

"But I didn't walk—no. I rode. I have ridden ever since. I sold one picture every day, and never tried to sell two. I always said to my customer:

I am a fool to sell a picture of François Millet's at all, for that man is not going to live three months, and when he dies his pictures can't be had for love or money.

"I took care to spread that little fact as far as I could, and prepare the world for the event. Claude and Carl were reporting equal success.

"Every now and then we got in with a country editor and started an item concerning the condition of the 'master' - always tinged with fears for the worst.

"Carl was soon in Paris and he made friends with the correspondents, and got Millet's condition reported all over the continent.

"At the end of six weeks, we three met in Paris and decided not to wait any longer. So we wrote Millet to go to bed and begin to waste away pretty fast, for we should like him to die in ten days.

"Then we figured up and found that among us we had sold eighty-five pictures, and had sixty-nine thousand francs to show for it.

"We had a champagne supper that night, and next day Claude and I went to nurse Millet through his last days and to send daily bulletins to Paris for publication in the papers of a waiting world.

"The sad end came at last, and Carl was there in time to help in the final mournful rites.

"You remember that great funeral, and what a stir it made all over the globe, and how the illustrious came to testify their sorrow."

We four carried the coffin, which hadn't anything in it but a wax figure, and—

But, which four?

We four. For Millet helped to carry his own coffin. In disguise as a distant relative.

Astonishing!

But true just the same. Well, you remember how the pictures went up. Money? We didn't know what to do with it. There's a man in Paris today who owns seventy Millet pictures. He paid us two million francs for them. And as for the bushels of sketches and studies which Millet shovelled out during the six weeks that we were on the road, well, it would astonish you to know the figures we sell them at nowadays!

Whatever became of Millet?

Can you keep a secret?

I can.

Do you remember the man I called your attention to earlier?

That was François Millet.

Great—

Scott! Yes. For once, this songbird was not allowed to pipe out its heart unheard and then be paid with the cold pomp of a big funeral. We looked out for that.

End

The Mysterious Stranger

by **Mark Twain**
adapted & illustrated by **Rick Geary**

It was 1590. It was still the Middle Ages in Austria, and promised to remain so forever.

Our village drowsed in a woodsy solitude, where news of the outside world hardly ever disturbed its dreams.

The whole region was the hereditary property of a prince, whose servants kept the castle in perfect condition, though he rarely visited there.

Eseldorf was a paradise for us boys. We were not overmuch pestered with schooling. Knowledge was not good for the common people, and could make them discontented with the lot which God had appointed for them.

We had two priests. Father Adolf was held in more solemn respect, because he had no fear at all of the Devil. This was known to be so, since Father Adolf had said it himself.

But it was Father Peter, the other priest, that we all loved best. But some people charged him with saying that God was all goodness and would find a way to save all his children.

It was a horrible thing to say, but there was never any proof that he had actually said it.

Father Peter had an enemy, and a very powerful one, the astrologer who lived in an old tower up the valley, and put in his nights studying the stars.

Everyone knew he could foretell wars and famines, though that was not so hard, for there was always a war, and generally a famine somewhere.

Everyone in the village except Father Peter stood in awe of him.

Father Peter denounced the astrologer openly as a charlatan, which made the astrologer hate Father Peter and wish to ruin him.

It was the astrologer, as we all believed, who originated the story about Father Peter's shocking remark and carried it to the bishop. The bishop suspended Father Peter indefinitely, though he wouldn't go so far as to excommunicate him.

Those had been hard years for the old priest and his niece, Marget. Many of their friends fell away entirely, and the rest became cool and distant.

Marget was a lovely girl of eighteen when the trouble came, and she had the best head in the village. She taught the harp, but her scholars fell off one by one.

The young fellows also stopped coming to the house, all except Wilhelm Meidling, who remained loyal.

Matters went worse and worse, all through the two years. And now, at last, the very end was come. Solomon Isaacs, the banker, gave notice that tomorrow he would foreclose on the house.

Three of us boys were always together, and had been so from the cradle –

Nikolaus Bauman, son of the local judge.

Seppi Wohlmeyer, son of the innkeeper.

And I was the third – Theodor Fischer.

We knew the hills and the woods and were always roaming them when we had leisure. One May morning we went up into the hills, and there we stretched out on the grass in the shade to rest and smoke and talk.

Soon there came a youth strolling toward us through the trees.

He sat down and began to talk in a friendly way, just as if he knew us. He was handsome, and wore new clothes.

I offered our pipe to him, but then I remembered that we had no fire.

FIRE? OH, I WILL FURNISH IT.

I was astonished, for I had not said anything.

He took the pipe and blew on it.

We jumped up and were going to run, but he pleaded with us to stay, giving his word that he only wanted to be friends with us.

He was bent on putting us at ease, and before long we were comfortable and chatty. He said such tricks came natural to him.

LET US SEE ANOTHER!

WITH PLEASURE.

He said he would give us any kind of fruit we liked, whether it was in season or not.

ORANGE!

APPLE!

GRAPES!

THEY ARE IN YOUR POCKETS,

AND EVERYTHING ELSE YOUR APPETITES CALL FOR— AS LONG AS I AM WITH YOU, YOU HAVE ONLY TO WISH.

He did one curious thing after another to amuse us.

He made a tiny squirrel out of clay, and it ran up a tree.

Then he made a toy dog that barked at the squirrel.

He made clay birds and they flew away, singing.

At last I asked him to tell us who he was.

AN ANGEL.

A kind of awe fell upon us, but he said we need not be afraid of an angel.

He went on chatting, and while he talked he made a crowd of little men and women, no bigger than your finger.

They went diligently to work and cleared a space in the grass and began to build a little castle.

Five hundred of these toy people swarming about and wiping the sweat off their faces as natural as life.

TELL US—
WHAT IS YOUR NAME?

SATAN.

111

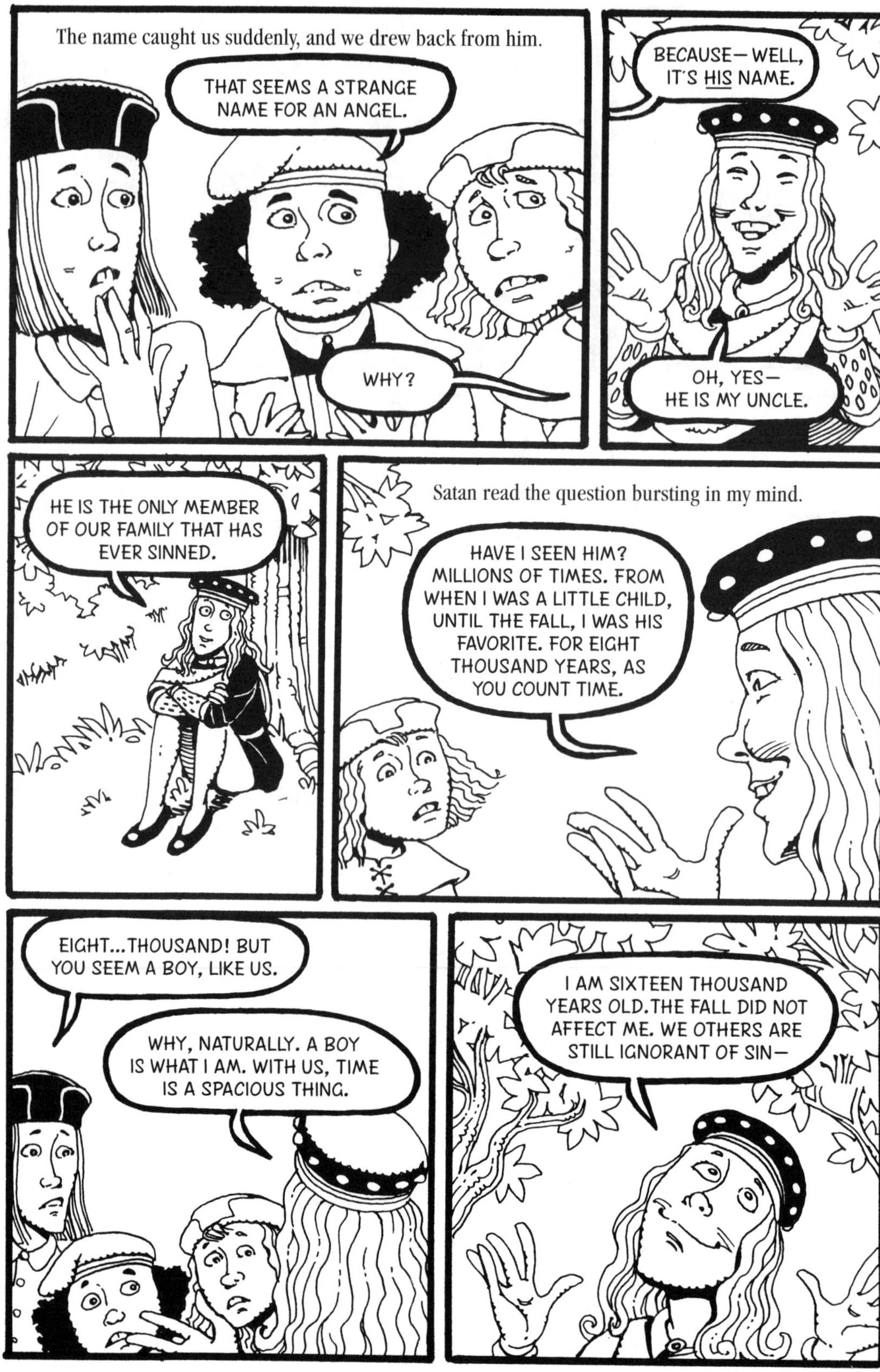
The name caught us suddenly, and we drew back from him.
THAT SEEMS A STRANGE NAME FOR AN ANGEL.
WHY?
BECAUSE—WELL, IT'S HIS NAME.
OH, YES—HE IS MY UNCLE.
HE IS THE ONLY MEMBER OF OUR FAMILY THAT HAS EVER SINNED.
Satan read the question bursting in my mind.
HAVE I SEEN HIM? MILLIONS OF TIMES. FROM WHEN I WAS A LITTLE CHILD, UNTIL THE FALL, I WAS HIS FAVORITE. FOR EIGHT THOUSAND YEARS, AS YOU COUNT TIME.
EIGHT...THOUSAND! BUT YOU SEEM A BOY, LIKE US.
WHY, NATURALLY. A BOY IS WHAT I AM. WITH US, TIME IS A SPACIOUS THING.
I AM SIXTEEN THOUSAND YEARS OLD.THE FALL DID NOT AFFECT ME. WE OTHERS ARE STILL IGNORANT OF SIN—

He was interrupted by two of the little workmen, who were quarreling. In buzzing little voices they were cursing each other.

Satan reached out his hand and crushed the life out of them with his fingers.

We were shocked at the murder he had committed.

But he went right on talking, as if nothing had happened.

WE ANGELS CAN DO NO WRONG, FOR WE KNOW NOT WHAT IT IS.

Now the wives of the little dead men had found the crushed bodies and were crying over them.

Satan paid no attention until the noise of the weeping and praying began to annoy him.

Then he reached out and took the heavy board seat out of our swing and mashed all those people into the earth just as if they had been flies!

It made us sick to see that awful deed.

But he went on talking right along, and worked his enchantments on us. He made us forget everything, and we could only listen and love him.

The Stranger had been everywhere, he had seen everything, and he forgot nothing. He had seen the world made; he had seen Adam created; he had seen the damned writhing in hell; and he made us see all these things.

He told us his real name was to be known to us alone. He had chosen another one to be called by in the presence of others—Philip Traum.

We had seen wonders this day; and my thoughts began to run on the pleasure it would be to tell of them.

NO, THESE MATTERS ARE A SECRET AMONG US. I WILL PROTECT YOUR TONGUES, AND NOTHING WILL ESCAPE.

FATHER PETER IS COMING. SIT STILL, AND BE QUIET.

I CAN'T THINK WHY I AM HERE; I WAS IN MY STUDY A MINUTE AGO — BUT I AM NOT MYSELF THESE DAYS.

He walked straight through Satan, just as if nothing were there.

I TOLD YOU — I AM BUT A SPIRIT.

Then he chatted along the same as ever. He spoke of men in the same way that one speaks of bricks and manure piles. I asked what was the difference between men and himself.

THE DIFFERENCE? MAN IS MADE OF DIRT. HE COMES TODAY AND IS GONE TOMORROW.

AND MAN HAS THE MORAL SENSE. THAT IS ENOUGH DIFFERENCE BETWEEN US, ALL BY ITSELF.

I had a dim idea of what the Moral Sense was. But I knew that we were proud of it.

I AM GOING NOW, BUT I WILL BE BACK.

Then he vanished.

I SUPPOSE NONE OF IT HAPPENED.

It was the same fear that was in my own mind. Then we saw Father Peter wandering back.

MAYBE YOU BOYS CAN HELP ME. I HAVE LOST MY WALLET. IT WAS ALL THAT I HAD.

WE WILL HELP LOOK.

HERE IT IS!

There it lay, right where Satan had vanished.

IT IS MINE, BUT NOT THESE. WHO HAS BEEN HERE?

The wallet was stuffed full with gold coins.

We all tried to say "Satan did it!" But we couldn't say his name.

NO HUMAN BEING.

WE SAW NO MAN.

IT'S ELEVEN HUNDRED DUCATS! IF IT WERE ONLY MINE—I NEED IT SO!

IT IS YOURS, SIR!

NO—IT ISN'T MINE. ONLY FOUR DUCATS.

WE ARE WITNESSES, FATHER PETER.

WE'LL STAND BY IT, TOO.

BLESS YOUR HEARTS, YOU ALMOST PERSUADE ME. IF I HAD ONLY A HUNDRED-ODD DUCATS OF IT...

IT'S YOURS, ALL OF IT, AND YOU MUST TAKE IT.

Finally, he said he would use two hundred of it, to save his house, and would put the rest at interest until the rightful owner came for it.

And we boys must sign a paper to prove that he had not got out of his troubles dishonestly.

It made much talk when Father Peter paid the mortgage in gold.

There was a pleasant change, and many old friends called at the house to congratulate him.

The old priest told the story just as it had happened, and said he could not account for it, only it was the hand of Providence.

One or two shook their heads and said privately it looked more like the hand of Satan, and tried to coax us boys to come out and "tell the truth."

There was a question which we wanted to ask Father Peter.

WHAT IS THE MORAL SENSE?

WHY, IT IS THE FACULTY WHICH ENABLES US TO TELL GOOD FROM EVIL.

IS IT VALUABLE?

VALUABLE?! IT IS THE ONE THING THAT LIFTS MAN ABOVE THE BEASTS AND MAKES HIM HEIR TO IMMORTALITY!

We passed through the parlor, and there was Marget, teaching Marie Lueger. Other pupils would follow.

And in the garden, Wilhelm Meidling waited. The young lawyer's faithfulness was not lost on Marget and her uncle.

On the fourth day came the astrologer from his crumbling old tower and had a private talk with us.

HOW MANY DUCATS WAS IT?

ELEVEN HUNDRED.

A CURIOUS COINCIDENCE. I KNOW THE THIEF NOW. THE MONEY WAS STOLEN.

Then he went away, leaving us wondering what he could mean.

In about an hour we found out; for it was all over the village that Father Peter had been arrested for stealing a great sum of money from the astrologer.

Many said it must be a mistake; but the others shook their heads and said misery and want could drive a man to almost anything.

Our characters began to suffer now. We were Father Peter's only witnesses; how much did he pay us to back up his fantastic tale?

Our fathers said we were disgracing our families, and our mothers begged us to save our families from shame.

We tried to tell the whole thing, Satan and all—but it wouldn't come out.

Father Peter was in prison, and the court would not sit for some time to come.

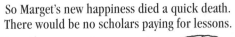

So Marget's new happiness died a quick death. There would be no scholars paying for lessons.

Ursula, who was housekeeper, said God would provide. But she meant to help in the providing.

On the fourth day after the catastrophe, I was out walking when a tingling sensation went rippling through me, and I knew that Satan was nearby.

Next moment he was alongside of me and I told him what had been happening to Marget and her uncle.

We saw Ursula resting in the shade of a tree, and she had a stray kitten in her lap.

I asked her where she got it.

IT CAME OUT OF THE WOODS AND FOLLOWED ME. I SUPPOSE I MUST LET IT GO, THOUGH IT WOULD BE SUCH PLEASANT COMPANY.

YOU SHOULD KEEP IT. THIS BREED BRINGS LUCK.

IS IT TRUE?

WELL, IT BRINGS MONEY, ANYWAY.

MONEY? PEOPLE DO NOT BUY CATS; ONE CAN'T GIVE THEM AWAY.

I DON'T MEAN SELL IT. THIS IS A LUCKY CAT. ITS OWNER FINDS FOUR SILVER GROSCHEN IN HIS POCKET EVERY MORNING.

I saw the indignation rising in Ursula's face. This boy was making fun of her. She thrust her hands into her pockets.

IT'S TRUE— IT'S TRUE!

Ursula started homeward, with the kitten in her arms.

I said I wished I had her privilege of seeing Marget.

Then I caught my breath, for we were there in the parlor, and Marget looking at us, astonished.

I introduced Satan— that is, Philip Traum – and we were soon friends.

Marget couldn't keep her eyes off him, he was so beautiful.

He said he was an orphan, but he had a wealthy uncle in business down in the tropics.

I HOPE OUR UNCLES MEET SOME DAY.

I HOPE SO, TOO.

The possibility made me shudder, but they chatted on, and poor Marget forgot her sorrow for a little while.

He promised to get her admitted to the jail to visit her uncle.

ALWAYS GO IN THE EVENING AFTER DARK, AND SHOW THIS PAPER AS YOU PASS IN.

I judged that the marks on the paper were an enchantment, and that the guards would not know what they were doing, nor remember afterward.

Ursula entered to announce supper.

Then she saw us and looked frightened, and motioned me to come.

HAVE YOU TOLD MISS MARGET ABOUT THE CAT?

NO, WE HAVEN'T.

PLEASE DON'T; FOR SHE WOULD THINK IT UNHOLY, AND SEND FOR A PRIEST.

I was beginning to say goodbye to Marget, but Satan interrupted and ever so politely invited himself to supper, and me, too.

Marget was embarrassed, for she knew they did not have enough, and Ursula seemed not a bit pleased.

I TOLD YOU, IT IS A LUCKY CAT. IT WILL PROVIDE.

And so it did: an abundance of fish and game and wines and fruits; and Satan talked right along and made the time pass pleasantly.

When it was dark, Marget took food and wine in a basket and hurried to the jail.

I was thinking that I should like to see what the inside of the jail was like. Satan heard the thought, and the next moment we were in the torture chamber. The people there took no notice of us, as we were invisible.

A young man lay bound, and Satan said he was suspected of being a heretic.

CONFESS TO THE CHARGE!

BUT IT IS NOT TRUE!

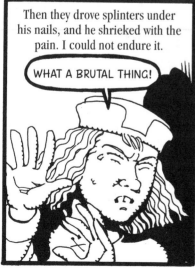

Then they drove splinters under his nails, and he shrieked with the pain. I could not endure it.

WHAT A BRUTAL THING!

NO, IT WAS A HUMAN THING. ONLY MAN INFLICTS PAIN FOR THE PLEASURE OF INFLICTING IT, INSPIRED BY THAT MORAL SENSE OF HIS!

I WILL SHOW YOU MORE.

In a moment we were in a French village. We walked through a great factory, where men and women and little children were toiling.

THE PROPRIETORS ARE RICH, BUT THE WAGE THEY PAY IS ONLY ENOUGH TO KEEP THESE PEOPLE FROM DROPPING DEAD WITH HUNGER.

YOU HAVE SEEN HOW THEY TREAT A MISDOER THERE IN THE JAIL; NOW YOU SEE HOW THEY TREAT THE INNOCENT.

IT IS THE MORAL SENSE WHICH TEACHES THE OWNERS THE DIFFERENCE BETWEEN RIGHT AND WRONG — YOU PERCEIVE THE RESULT.

Then he overstrained himself making fun of us, and deriding our pride in our great heroes and our venerable history.

BUT, AFTER ALL, THERE IS A SORT OF PATHOS ABOUT IT WHEN ONE REMEMBERS HOW FEW ARE YOUR DAYS.

The next moment we were back in our village. I heard a joyful cry: It was Seppi Wohlmeyer.

YOU'VE COME AGAIN!

Seppi was full of the latest mystery— the disappearance of Hans Oppert, the village loafer.

NO ONE HAS SEEN HIM SINCE HE DID THAT BRUTAL THING.

WHAT THING?

WELL, HE WAS ALWAYS CLUBBING HIS DOG, AND TWO DAYS AGO HE STRUCK THE DOG WITH ALL HIS MIGHT AND KNOCKED ONE OF HIS EYES OUT. AND THEN HE LAUGHED, THE HEARTLESS BRUTE.

THERE IS THAT WORD AGAIN. BRUTES DO NOT ACT LIKE THAT, ONLY MEN.

Soon that poor dog came along, with his eye hanging down. It went straight to Satan and began to moan, and Satan answered, and it was plain that they were talking together in the dog language. Satan took the dog's head in his lap and put the eye back in its place, and the dog wagged his tail and licked Satan's hand.

HE SAYS HIS MASTER WAS DRUNK, AND HE FELL OVER A CLIFF.

THE DOG HAS BEEN BEGGING FOR HELP, BUT HE WAS ONLY DRIVEN AWAY. HE ONLY WANTED TO AID THE MAN WHO HAS MISTREATED HIM.

IS HEAVEN RESERVED FOR YOUR RACE, AND THIS DOG RULED OUT, AS YOUR TEACHERS TELL YOU?

We got some men and found the body. Nobody cared but the dog. He licked the dead face and could not be comforted.

There was a very dull week, now, for Satan did not come, and our parents forbade us to see Marget.

But we saw Ursula a couple of times. She bore a prosperous look.

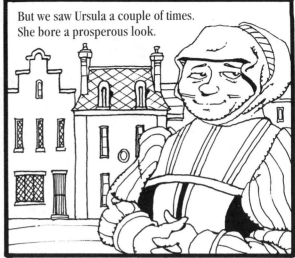

She said Marget spent an hour or two every night in the jail, and was enduring her isolation fairly well, with the help of Wilhelm Meidling.

The astrologer reported Marget and Ursula's new prosperity to Father Adolf.

THERE MUST BE WITCHCRAFT AT THE BOTTOM OF IT.

The priest told the villagers to resume relations with Marget and report to him.

YOU WILL BE UNDER MY PROTECTION FROM EVIL.

And so poor Marget began to have company again. The cat began to strain itself, providing for all the visitors.

Marget knew that nothing was impossible to Providence, but she could not help doubting that this effort was from there.

Marget announced a party, and invited forty people. The guests filled the place. Father Adolf arrived, and soon after him, the astrologer, without invitation.

Satan came, as well.

He apologized for intruding, but Marget brought him in and introduced him to the guests.

There was quite a rustle of whispers among the girls.

The astrologer had drunk his second beaker of wine and poured out a third. when he noticed something.

He called for a large bowl and began to pour wine into it. He poured until the bowl was filled to the brim.

Yet the bottle remained full!

Father Adolf rose up, excited.

THIS HOUSE IS ACCURSED! I SUMMON THIS DETECTED HOUSEHOLD TO —

His words were cut short. His face became red, then purple, but he could not utter another sound.

The people began to cry and shriek and crowd toward the door.

Then I saw Satan melt into the astrologer's body.

WAIT — DON'T RUN!

He called for a funnel.

Then he took up the great bowl and poured all the wine back into the bottle.

IT IS NOTHING — WITH MY POWERS I CAN DO MUCH MORE!

MY GOD, HE IS POSSESSED!

The astrologer then strode from the house, as the crowd followed him at a distance.

When he reached the market square he went up to a juggler.

THIS CLOWN IS IGNORANT OF HIS ART. WATCH AN EXPERT PERFORM.

So saying, he tossed the balls up and set them whirling in the air.

He added another, and another, his hands moving so swiftly that they were just a blur.

Then he turned and saw the tightrope, and said now the people should see the work of a master.

He sprang into the air and lit on the tightrope. He hopped the length of it on one foot, then began to throw somersaults.

Finally he sprang lightly down and disappeared up the road.

WAS IT REAL?

OR WAS IT ALL A DREAM?

I returned to Marget's house, where it was like a funeral.

I HAVE BEEN BEGGING HIM TO GO, AND SO SAVE HIMSELF.

I WILL NOT GO. IF THERE IS DANGER, MY PLACE IS BY YOU.

There was a knock, and Satan came in and changed the mood.

He said not a word about what had happened, but instead rattled on about all manner of pleasant things.

Marget was charmed, but Wilhelm did not look pleased.

Late that night, Satan roused me from sleep.

WHERE SHALL WE GO?

ANYWHERE.

There was a fierce glare of sunlight, and we were over a strange land.

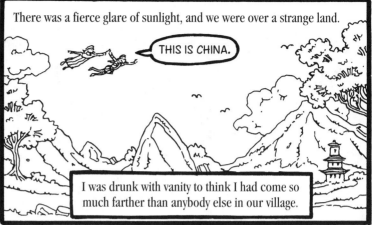

THIS IS CHINA.

I was drunk with vanity to think I had come so much farther than anybody else in our village.

Finally, we lit upon a mountaintop. As we talked, I had the idea of trying to reform Satan.

I KNOW YOU DO NOT MEAN ANY HARM, BUT YOU OUGHT TO STOP AND CONSIDER THE CONSEQUENCES OF A THING BEFORE DOING IT.

BUT I KNOW WHAT THE CONSEQUENCES ARE GOING TO BE—ALWAYS.

THEN HOW CAN YOU DO THESE THINGS?

WELL, YOU MUST UNDERSTAND IF YOU CAN.

MEN HAVE NOTHING IN COMMON WITH ME. MY MIND CREATES ANYTHING IT DESIRES—AND IN A MOMENT.

WE ANGELS CANNOT LOVE MEN, BUT WE CAN LIKE THEM. AND FOR YOUR SAKE I AM DOING THESE THINGS FOR THE VILLAGERS.

He saw that I was thinking a sarcasm, and he explained.

WHAT I AM DOING FOR THE VILLAGERS WILL BEAR GOOD FRUIT TO UNBORN GENERATIONS OF MEN.

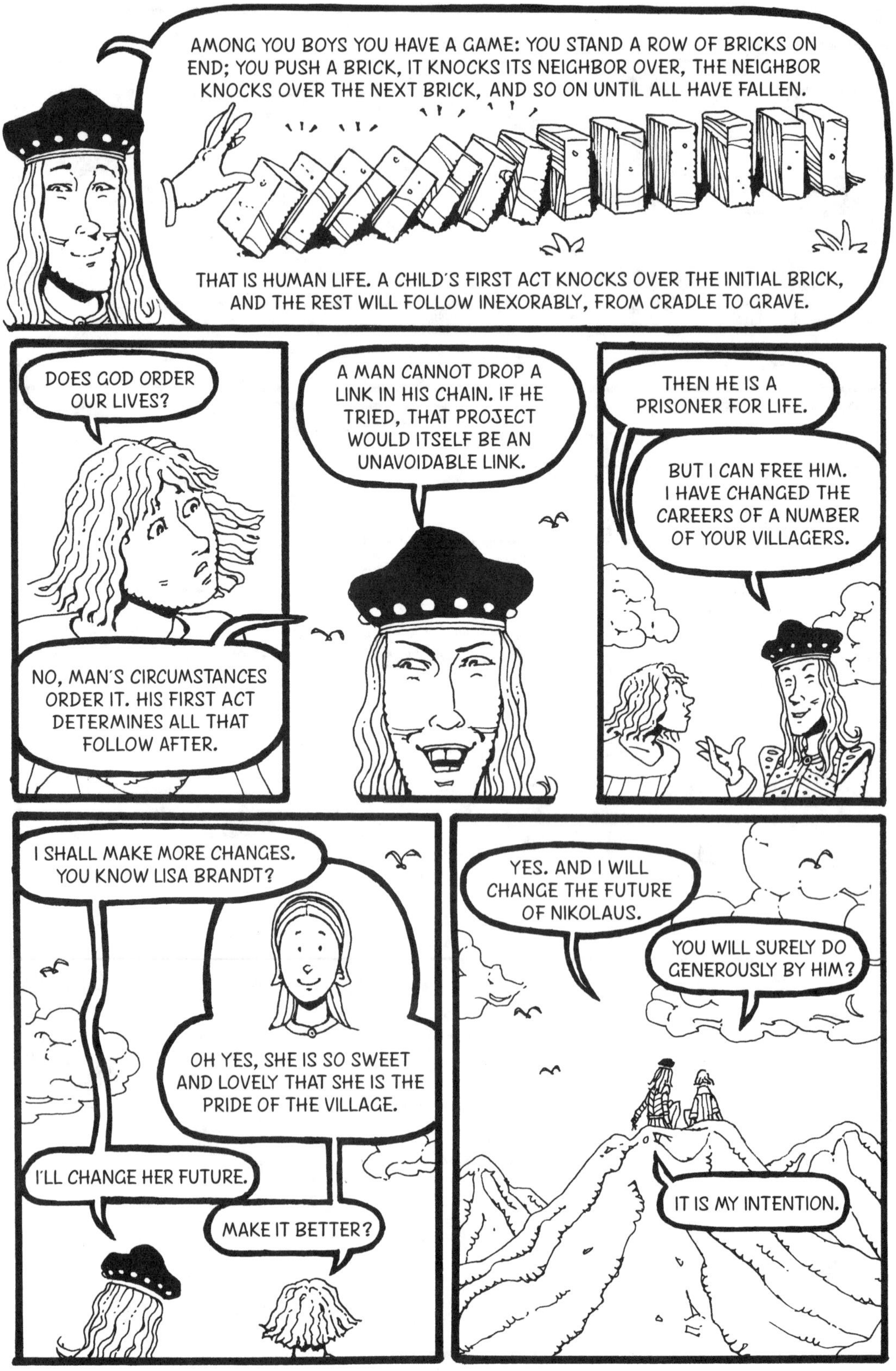
AMONG YOU BOYS YOU HAVE A GAME: YOU STAND A ROW OF BRICKS ON END; YOU PUSH A BRICK, IT KNOCKS ITS NEIGHBOR OVER, THE NEIGHBOR KNOCKS OVER THE NEXT BRICK, AND SO ON UNTIL ALL HAVE FALLEN.
THAT IS HUMAN LIFE. A CHILD'S FIRST ACT KNOCKS OVER THE INITIAL BRICK, AND THE REST WILL FOLLOW INEXORABLY, FROM CRADLE TO GRAVE.
DOES GOD ORDER OUR LIVES?
NO, MAN'S CIRCUMSTANCES ORDER IT. HIS FIRST ACT DETERMINES ALL THAT FOLLOW AFTER.
A MAN CANNOT DROP A LINK IN HIS CHAIN. IF HE TRIED, THAT PROJECT WOULD ITSELF BE AN UNAVOIDABLE LINK.
THEN HE IS A PRISONER FOR LIFE.
BUT I CAN FREE HIM. I HAVE CHANGED THE CAREERS OF A NUMBER OF YOUR VILLAGERS.
I SHALL MAKE MORE CHANGES. YOU KNOW LISA BRANDT?
OH YES, SHE IS SO SWEET AND LOVELY THAT SHE IS THE PRIDE OF THE VILLAGE.
I'LL CHANGE HER FUTURE.
MAKE IT BETTER?
YES. AND I WILL CHANGE THE FUTURE OF NIKOLAUS.
YOU WILL SURELY DO GENEROUSLY BY HIM?
IT IS MY INTENTION.

NICKY'S APPOINTED LIFE IS SIXTY-TWO YEARS. LISA'S, THIRTY-SIX. BUT I SHALL CHANGE THOSE AGES.

THAT'S GRAND!

TWO MINUTES FROM NOW NIKOLAUS WILL WAKE AND FIND THE RAIN BLOWING IN. IT WAS APPOINTED THAT HE SHOULD TURN OVER AND GO TO SLEEP AGAIN. BUT NOW HE SHALL GET UP AND CLOSE THE WINDOW FIRST.

BY CONSEQUENCE, THENCEFORTH NOTHING WILL EVER HAPPEN TO HIM IN ACCORDANCE WITH THE OLD CHAIN OF HIS LIFE.

It made me feel creepy to hear him say that.

BUT FOR THIS CHANGE, CERTAIN THINGS WOULD HAPPEN TWELVE DAYS FROM NOW. NIKOLAUS WOULD SAVE LISA FROM DROWNING. HE WOULD ARRIVE ON THE SCENE AT EXACTLY THE RIGHT MOMENT— FOUR MINUTES PAST TEN.

BUT NOW HE WILL ARRIVE SOME SECONDS TOO LATE.

LISA WILL HAVE STRUGGLED INTO DEEPER WATER. NICKY WILL DO HIS BEST, BUT BOTH WILL DROWN.

OH, SATAN! DON'T LET IT HAPPEN!

BUT IF I HAD NOT DONE THIS, NIKOLAUS WOULD SAVE LISA. THEN HE WOULD CATCH COLD, AND SCARLET FEVER WOULD FOLLOW. FOR FORTY-SIX YEARS HE WOULD LIE IN HIS BED, PRAYING FOR THE RELIEF OF DEATH. SHALL I CHANGE HIS LIFE BACK?

OH NO! IN PITY LEAVE IT AS IT IS.

I COULD NOT HAVE CHANGED ANY OTHER THING AND DONE HIM SO GOOD A SERVICE.

I wondered about poor little Lisa's fate.

SHE ESCAPES TEN YEARS OF PAINFUL RECOVERY, THEN NINETEEN OF SHAME AND DEPRAVITY, ENDING WITH DEATH AT THE HANDS OF THE EXECUTIONER.

PLEASE, NO.

BUT I CAN HELP FATHER PETER. HE WILL BE ACQUITTED, HIS GOOD NAME RESTORED, AND THE REST OF HIS LIFE WILL BE HAPPY.

That reminded me of the astrologer, and I wondered where he might be.

ON THE MOON. I'VE GOT HIM ON THE COLD SIDE OF IT, TOO. BUT I AM QUITE WILLING TO DO HIM A KINDNESS — I THINK I SHALL GET HIM BURNED.

He had a strange notion of kindness! But the ways of angels are not ours.

Satan returned me to my bed, but sleep would not come. My mind was filled with Nikolaus, and our days together.

In the morning I sought out Seppi and told him.

LESS THAN TWELVE DAYS?

We walked up among the hills and talked about our times with Nikolaus.

WE MUST BE WITH HIM ALL THE TIME; THESE DAYS ARE PRECIOUS.

It was a shock when we turned a curve and came upon Nikolaus face to face.

YOU LOOK LIKE YOU'VE SEEN A GHOST!

We wandered with him for many a mile, as we talked about old times.

Our tone toward him was so gentle that he noticed it, and was pleased.

We spent all of our spare time with Nikolaus. He was happy, but always puzzled because we were not.

When the evening of the last day came we stayed out too long. Seppi and I were in fault for that, for we could not bear to part with our friend.

In the morning, we went to his home. His mother met us at the door.

HIS FATHER IS OUT OF PATIENCE WITH THESE GOINGS-ON. NICKY GOT A FLOGGING FOR BEING LATE LAST NIGHT.

I AM SORRY, BUT HE CANNOT GO OUT OF THE HOUSE TODAY.

We had a great hope. If he could not leave the house, he could not be drowned!

She allowed us to go upstairs to visit Nikolaus.

We both noticed the time— a quarter to ten. Only such a few minutes to live!

SIT DOWN. I'VE FINISHED A KITE THAT IS DRYING IN THE KITCHEN. I'LL FETCH IT.

Then he went clattering down the stairs, as we sat and watched the clock.

THEODOR, HE WILL BE SAVED!

Then his mother entered, bringing the kite.

BUT WHERE IS NICKY?

HE'LL BE HERE SOON; HE'S OUT FOR A MINUTE.

HE'S OUTSIDE?

YES. LITTLE LISA'S MOTHER CAME IN AND SAID THE CHILD HAD WANDERED OFF SOME-WHERE. I TOLD NIKOLAUS TO GO OUT AND LOOK FOR HER.

We hurried to the window and looked toward the river.

IT IS ALL OVER! POOR NIKOLAUS!

Presently the thing happened which we were dreading. A crowd came solemnly in, and laid the two drowned bodies on the bed.

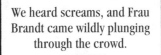

OH, IF ONLY I HAD KEPT HIM IN THE HOUSE, THIS WOULD NOT HAVE HAPPENED!

We heard screams, and Frau Brandt came wildly plunging through the crowd.

FOR TWO WEEKS I HAVE HAD DREAMS THAT DEATH WOULD STRIKE THAT MOST PRECIOUS TO ME.

AND DAY AND NIGHT I HAVE GROVELED IN THE DIRT, PRAYING FOR HIS PITY— AND HERE IS HIS ANSWER. I WILL NEVER PRAY AGAIN!

Both funerals took place the next day.

Everybody was there, even Satan; which was proper, for it was on account of him that the funerals had happened.

At the graveyard, the body of little Lisa was seized for debt by a carpenter to whom the mother owed fifty groschen.

He took the corpse home and kept it four days, then he buried it without ceremony in his brother's cattle-yard.

This drove the mother wild with grief and shame, and it was pitiful to see.

We begged Satan to examine the woman's possible careers, and see if he could not change her to a new one.

HER PATH IS CHARGED WITH GRIEF AND PAIN. THE ONLY IMPROVEMENT I COULD MAKE WOULD BE A CERTAIN THREE MINUTES FROM NOW.

DO IT!

IT IS DONE.

SHE IS NOW HAVING WORDS WITH FISCHER, THE WEAVER. IN HIS ANGER HE WILL BETRAY HER FOR THE BLASPHEMIES SHE SAID OVER HER CHILD'S BODY. IN THREE DAYS SHE WILL GO TO THE STAKE.

We were frozen with horror. Satan could not seem to do any person a kindness but by killing him.

BUT BY THIS PROMPT DEATH THE WOMAN GETS TWENTY-NINE YEARS MORE OF HEAVEN AND ESCAPES TWENTY-NINE YEARS OF MISERY HERE.

The trial was crowded. Frau Brandt's was easily convicted of her blas-phemies, for she said she would not take them back.

TAKE MY LIFE, AND WELCOME! I WOULD RATHER LIVE WITH THE REAL DEVILS IN PERDITION THAN WITH YOU IMITATORS.

They found her guilty, and she was sentenced and excommunicated.

We saw her chained to the stake, and we walked away and did not see the fires consume her, but we heard the shrieks.

When they ceased we knew she was in heaven, notwithstanding the excommunication; and we were not sorry that we had caused her death.

One day, a little while after this, Satan appeared again at the place where we had first met him. We asked him to do a show for us.

I WILL SHOW YOU THE PROGRESS OF HUMAN CIVILIZATION.

He showed us the Garden of Eden, and Cain's murder of Abel.

The vision was followed by a long series of wars, murders, massacres and hideous drenchings of blood.

We saw Caesar invade Britain.

HE WANTED TO CONFER THE BLESSINGS OF CIVILIZATION ON THE WIDOWS AND ORPHANS.

YOU HAVE MADE CONTINUAL PROGRESS. CAIN DID HIS MURDER WITH A CLUB; THE ROMANS WITH SWORDS; THE CHRISTIAN HAS ADDED GUNS.

WITHOUT CHRISTIAN CIVILIZATION, WAR MUST HAVE REMAINED A TRIFLING THING.

We saw Christianity and Civilization march hand in hand through the ages, leaving famine and death and desolation in their wake.

FOR A MILLION YEARS YOUR RACE HAS RE-PERFORMED THIS DULL NONSENSE— TO WHAT END?

WHO GETS A PROFIT OUT OF IT? NOBODY BUT A PARCEL OF USURPING LITTLE MONARCHS WHO DESPISE YOU — BUT WHOM YOU CONTINUE TO FIGHT AND DIE FOR.

We were hurt by Satan's words, but we did not know how to answer him.

Poor Seppi looked distressed, and I was deeply depressed.

Meanwhile, our people were witch-hunting. They caught a lady who was known to have the habit of curing people by devilish arts, such as bathing and nourishing them instead of bleeding them in the proper way.

They dragged her to a tree to be hanged.

As she passed me, I threw a stone, although in my heart I was sorry for her.

But all were throwing stones and if I had not done as the others did, it would have been noticed.

Satan burst out laughing.

IN FEAR, YOU STONED THE WOMAN WHEN YOUR HEART REVOLTED AT THE ACT. OH, BUT YOUR RACE IS MADE UP OF SHEEP!

GOVERNMENTS, ARISTOCRACIES, AND RELIGIONS ARE ALL BASED UPON THAT LARGE DEFECT IN YOUR RACE— MAN'S DISTRUST OF HIS NEIGHBOR, AND HIS DESIRE TO STAND WELL IN HIS NEIGHBOR'S EYE.

With that, Satan vanished. The following days were dull without him.

At last, Father Peter's trial came, and people gathered from all around to witness it. Marget asked Wilhelm Meidling to defend her uncle.

If Satan would only come! Of course I did not doubt that the case would be won, and that Father Peter would be happy for the rest of his life, since Satan had said so.

Everybody was there except the accused. He was too feeble for the strain.

The money was emptied on a table, and was examined by such as were privileged.

138

The astrologer, returned from the moon, was put in the witness-box.

HOW DID YOU COME BY THIS MONEY YOU CLAIM IS YOURS?

I FOUND THE BAG IN THE ROAD WHEN I WAS ON A JOURNEY.

WHEN?

IT WAS MORE THAN TWO YEARS AGO.

WHAT DID YOU DO?

I BROUGHT IT HOME AND HID IT IN A SECRET PLACE IN MY OBSERVATORY, INTENDING TO FIND THE OWNER IF I COULD.

SOME TIME LATER, I TOOK IT OUT AND COUNTED IT. AND THEN... I AM SORRY TO HAVE TO SAY THIS, BUT JUST AS I HAD FINISHED, I LOOKED UP AND THERE STOOD FATHER PETER BEHIND ME.

AFTER I HEARD OF FATHER PETER'S FIND I CAME HOME AND DISCOVERED THAT MY OWN MONEY WAS GONE. HE HAD FOUND EXACTLY THE SAME SUM AS I HAD LOST.

Wilhelm Meidling then called us boys, and we told our tale.

It might be difficult for people to believe the astrologer's story, considering his character, but it was almost impossible to believe ours.

The astrologer's lawyer made a sarcastic little speech that made everybody laugh at us.

And at last Marget could no longer keep up her courage but broke down and cried.

Then I saw something that braced me up. Satan was standing alongside of Wilhelm! No one else noticed Satan, so I knew that he was invisible.

Satan then began to melt into Wilhelm, and his spirit looked out of the lawyer's eyes.

He then confronted the accuser.

YOU HAVE TESTIFIED THAT YOU FOUND THIS MONEY MORE THAN TWO YEARS AGO.

THAT IS CORRECT.

AND THE MONEY WAS NEVER OUT OF YOUR HANDS UP TO THE LAST DAY OF LAST YEAR?

ALSO CORRECT.

IF I PROVE THE MONEY HERE IS NOT THAT HE FOUND, THEN IT IS NOT HIS?

CERTAINLY NOT; BUT IF YOU HAVE A NEW WITNESS YOU MUST GIVE PROPER NOTICE.

BUT I SPEAK OF THE COIN ITSELF. IT WAS NOT IN EXISTENCE LAST DECEMBER. OBSERVE THE DATES.

ALL OF THE COINS ARE OF THIS PRESENT YEAR. THE COURT TENDERS ITS SINCERE SYMPATHY TO THE ACCUSED. THE CASE IS DISMISSED!

Everybody rushed forward to congratulate Marget and Wilhelm.

Satan was gone. I judged that he had spirited himself away to the jail.

But Satan had told Father Peter that he stood disgraced as a thief – by verdict of the court!

The shock of this unseated the old priest's reason.

When we arrived, he was parading around and delivering commands. He thought he was the Emperor!

IT IS NOT BECOMING FOR THE CROWN PRINCESS TO CRY. JUST TELL ME YOUR TROUBLE AND IT SHALL BE MENDED!

Marget and Ursula walked him home, crying all the way. It was as pitiful a sight as ever I saw. I reproached Satan for deceiving me.

IT WAS THE TRUTH. I SAID HE WOULD BE HAPPY, AND HE IS NOW THE ONE UTTERLY HAPPY PERSON IN THIS EMPIRE.

NO SANE MAN CAN BE HAPPY. IT SEEMS TO ME THAT YOU ARE HARD TO PLEASE.

For a year Satan continued his visits, but then he came less often. When one day he finally visited, I was overjoyed.

OUR TIME TOGETHER HAS BEEN PLEASANT, BUT WE SHALL NOT SEE EACH OTHER ANY MORE.

BUT SURELY WE SHALL MEET IN ANOTHER LIFE, SATAN.

NO, THERE IS NO OTHER LIFE. IT IS NOT REAL!

So the afterlife is only a vision… a dream! I had held that very thought a thousand times!

GOD — MAN — THE WORLD — THE STARS ARE ALL A DREAM. AND I MYSELF AM BUT A CREATURE OF YOUR IMAGINATION!

STRANGE THAT YOU SHOULD NOT HAVE SUSPECTED AGES AGO, FOR YOUR UNIVERSE AND ITS CONTENTS ARE SO FRANKLY AND HYSTERICALLY INSANE.

A GOD WHO COULD MAKE EVERY PERSON HAPPY, YET GIVES THEM MISERIES AND MALADIES; WHO MOUTHS MERCY AND INVENTED HELL; WHO CREATED MAN WITHOUT INVITATION, THEN TRIES TO SHUFFLE THE RESPONSIBILITY FOR MAN'S ACTS UPON MAN; AND FINALLY REQUIRES THIS POOR, ABUSED SLAVE TO WORSHIP HIM! THESE THINGS ARE IMPOSSIBLE EXCEPT IN A HORRIBLE DREAM!

AND NOTHING EXISTS BUT YOU, A VAGRANT THOUGHT, WANDERING AMONG THE EMPTY ETERNITIES!

He vanished, and left me appalled; for I realized that all he had said was true.

Ende

MARK TWAIN

Born in Missouri in 1835, Samuel Langhorne Clemens took his pen name from the alert common among steamboat crews on his beloved Mississippi River for water "two fathoms deep." As a boy, he wanted to be a riverboat pilot, and became one, until the advent of the Civil War caused him, with his brother, to move to the Nevada Territory in 1861. He started as a newspaper reporter in Virginia City, and there wrote his first successful story, *The Celebrated Jumping Frog of Calaveras County*. He went on to become one of the most popular authors and humorists in American history. While today best known for what are taken as children's novels, *The Adventures of Tom Sawyer* and *The Adventures of Huckleberry Finn* as well as the lesser-known sequel, *Tom Sawyer Abroad*, Mark Twain also authored a vast range of novels, short stories, travel books, articles, essays and satirical sketches. Failed investments and the early deaths of his wife and daughters led to an increasingly cynical view in his later writings, including *The Mysterious Stranger*. He died at his home in Connecticut at age 75.

GEORGE SELLAS (cover, page 4)

George Sellas is a freelance cartoonist and illustrator from Cheshire, Connecticut. He is a graduate of Paier College of Art in Hamden, Connecticut with a BFA in Illustration. His work has appeared in *Highlights* magazine, in *How to Draw Those Bodacious Bad Babes of Comics* by Frank McLaughlin and Mike Gold, and in *Graphic Classics: Ambrose Bierce* and *Graphic Classics: Robert Louis Stevenson*. *Tom Sawyer Abroad* is his first full-length comics story. "I'm always looking for more work to whet my artistic appetite," says George. He is now working on an adaptation of Stanley Weinbaum's *A Martian Odyssey* for the upcoming *Science Fiction Classics*. You can get more info and view an extensive gallery of George's illustrations at www.georgesellas.com.

LISA K. WEBER (page 2)

Lisa is a graduate of Parsons School of Design in New York City, where she is currently employed in the fashion industry, designing prints and characters for teenage girls' jammies, while freelancing work on children's books and character design for animation. Other projects include her "creaturized" opera posters and playing cards. Lisa has provided illustrations for *Graphic Classics: Edgar Allan Poe*, *Graphic Classics: H.P. Lovecraft*, *Graphic Classics: Ambrose Bierce*, *Graphic Classics: Bram Stoker* and *Rosebud 25*. She adapted *The Gift of the Magi* in *Graphic Classics: O. Henry* and *Carmilla* for *Gothic Classics*. More of Lisa's work can be seen online at www.creatureco.com.

MARK DANCEY (page 3)

Mark Dancey was born in Ann Arbor, Michigan in 1963. "For no good reason," Mark co-founded the satirical and highly influential *Motorbooty*

Magazine in the late 1980s and filled its pages with his comics and illustrations. As a member of rock band Big Chief during the 1990s he got a lock on the position of band propagandist and subsequently produced all manner of CD covers, T-shirt designs, backdrops and posters for that outfit. Having extricated himself from the world of rock, Mark now lives in Detroit, where he produces painstaking works in oil and prints silk-screened posters under the aegis of his company, Illuminado.com. His work also appears in *Graphic Classics: Ambrose Bierce*.

KEVIN ATKINSON (back cover, page 41)

"I've lived in Texas my whole life with the exception of 1985–1988, when I went to New Jersey to study with [famed comics artist and teacher] Joe Kubert," says Kevin. Since then he has created short stories and full-length comics for various publishers. He wrote and drew two series, *Snarl* and *Planet 29*, and collaborated on another, *Rogue Satellite Comics*. He's inked *The Tick* comics, and illustrated Drew Edward's *Halloween Man*, *Sweet Ermengarde* for *Graphic Classics: H.P. Lovecraft* and *Some Words with a Mummy* for *Horror Classics*. Kevin also illustrated *Blood Money*, a Rafael Sabatini tale, for *Adventure Classics* and a biography of the author for *Graphic Classics: Rafael Sabatini*. Visit www.meobeco.com/pulptoons/index.htm to see more of his art.

LANCE TOOKS (page 53)

As an animator for fifteen years, as well as a comics artist, Lance Tooks' work has appeared in more than a hundred television commercials, films and music videos. He has self-published the comics *Divided by Infinity Danger Funnies* and *Muthafucka*. His stories have appeared in *Zuzu*, *Shade*, *Vibe*, *Girltalk*, *World War 3 Illustrated*, *Floaters*, *Pure Friction*, the Italian magazine *Lupo Alberto*, *Graphic Classics: Ambrose Bierce*, *Graphic Classics: Edgar Allan Poe* and *Graphic Classics: Robert Louis Stevenson*. He also illustrated *The Black Panthers for Beginners*, written by Herb Boyd. Lance's first graphic novel, *Narcissa*, was named one of the best books of 2002 by *Publisher's Weekly*, and he has recently completed his *Lucifer's Garden of Verses* series for NBM ComicsLit. In 2004 Lance moved from his native New York to Madrid, Spain, where he married and has just finished a Spanish translation of *Narcissa*.

FLORENCE CESTAC (page 68)

Born in 1949, Florence Cestac studied art in Rouen and Paris. She co-founded Bonbel, an artist collective in Rouen, and in 1972 she co-founded the bookstore Futuropolis and later a publishing company with the same name. Her comic character "Harry Mickson" became the company's emblem and mascot. Cestac's work has appeared in magazines including *Ah Nana!*, *Métal Hurlant*, *Charlie Mensuel*, *Pilote* and *Chic*, and in *Graphic Classics: Ambrose Bierce*. Her books include *Cauchemar*

Matinal, Comment Faire de la Bédé, La Guerre des Boutons, Le Démon de Midi, Je Veux Pas Divorcer and *Survivre & Noël.* Her comics autobiography *La Vie D'Artiste* was published in 2002 by Dargaud.

KIRSTEN ULVE (*page 69*)

Kirsten Ulve began her career as a graphic designer and part-time illustrator in Chicago, then relocated to New York in 1996 to devote herself to illustration full time. Since then she has worked in almost every arena of the field, ranging from fashion illustration to caricatures, animated commercials to advertising art, editorial illustration to product embellishment. Her clients include *Entertainment Weekly, Rolling Stone, Cosmogirl, Seventeen, The Village Voice, Nickelodeon,* Mattel, Popsicle, Hasbro and Palty of Japan. She has exhibited her work at the CWC Gallery in Tokyo, at Sixspace Gallery in Los Angeles and many others. You can find more of her work at www.kirstenulve.com.

SHARY FLENNIKEN (*page 70*)

Shary Flenniken is a cartoonist, editor, author and screenwriter. She is best known for her irreverent comic strip *Trots & Bonnie,* about precocious preteens, which appeared in various underground comics and *National Lampoon.* Shary's graphic stories and comic strips have appeared in *Details, Premiere, Harvey,* and *Mad* magazines, as well as in *Graphic Classics: Ambrose Bierce, Graphic Classics: O. Henry, Graphic Classics: Robert Louis Stevenson* and *Gothic Classics.* Her artwork can also be seen in *When a Man Loves A Walnut, More Misheard Lyrics* by the "very cool" Gavin Edwards, *Nice Guys Sleep Alone* by "big-time loser" Bruce Feirstein, and *Seattle Laughs,* a "truly wonderful" book edited by Shary. She is currently teaching comedy writing and cartooning while working on a book of fairy tales and a series of novels that she claims are "not even remotely autobiographical." You can contact Shary and find out how to purchase original artwork at www.sharyflenniken.com.

TONI PAWLOWSKY (*page 71*)

Toni is both an exhibiting fine artist and a commercial illustrator. She shows her watercolors at the Fanny Garver Gallery in Madison, WI, and is also represented by Langley and Associates in Chicago. Her commercial work includes numerous CD covers for the series *Music for Little People,* including two covers for Taj Mahal. She has done work for the Wisconsin Dance Ensemble and Madison Ballet. She was the featured artist in *Rosebud 17* and appears in *Graphic Classics: Edgar Allan Poe.* Her prints can be purchased at www.guild.com, her greeting cards are at www.redoakcards.com, and more art can be viewed at www.kookykool.com.

MARY FLEENER (*page 72*)

Besides doing comics, like her biweekly strip *Mary-Land,* autobiographical collection *Life of the Party,* and Eros title *Nipplez 'n' Tum Tum,* Los Angeles native Mary has also produced illustrations for magazines and books such as *Guitar Player, Musician, Spin, Hustler, The Book of Changes, Guitar Cookbook, RoadStrips,* and Poppy Z. Brite's *Plastic Jesus.* Her paintings have been shown at The American Visionary Art Museum, La Luz de Jesus Gallery, and the Laguna Beach Art Museum. She is currently painting on black velvet, and makes hand-thrown ceramics. Fleener also plays bass, and sings her own tunes in a band called The Wigbillies with her husband. She loves to surf, and walks a lot. Her art also appears in *Graphic Classics: Edgar Allan Poe* and *Adventure Classics.* Mary's website is at www.maryfleener.com.

ANNIE OWENS (*page 73*)

Annie was born in Alabama, "parcel posted to the Philippines," and after three years was returned to the States and educated in the San Francisco Bay area where she earned her BFA in film and video. She is a fan of old horror films, the art of Charles Addams and Edward Gorey and the writings of Roald Dahl, Edgar Allan Poe and H.P. Lovecraft. Her work appears in the Poe volume of *Graphic Classics,* and her adaptation of *Oil of Dog* appears in *Graphic Classics: Ambrose Bierce.* Samples of Annie's comic strip *Ouchclub* can be seen at www.ouchclub.com as well as in Attaboy's comic anthology, *I Hate Cartoons, Volume II.* With Attaboy she also co-edits *Hi-Fructose* magazine.

LESLEY REPPETEAUX (*page 74*)

Lesley (*aka* Black Olive) is a Los Angeles-based illustrator whose work has appeared in numerous publications including *Amplifier Magazine, Adventure Cyclist, Bitch, Delaware Today* and *Graphic Classics: Ambrose Bierce.* Between freelance assignments, she exhibits her paintings in galleries nationwide, and is the creative force behind *Outlook: Grim,* a spooky comic book series published by Slave Labor Graphics. Currently on the last leg of a year abroad, when she is "not overexerting herself or being a busy little bumblebee," she is updating her website, which you can check out at www.reppeteaux.com.

ANTONELLA CAPUTO (*page 75*)

Antonella was born and raised in Rome, Italy, and now lives in Lancaster, England. She has been an architect, archaeologist, art restorer, photographer, calligrapher, interior designer, theater designer, actress and theater director. Her first published work was *Casa Montesi,* a fortnightly comic strip which appeared in the national magazine *Il Giornalino.* She has since written comedies for children and scripts for comics and magazines in the UK, Europe and the U.S. She works with Nick Miller as the writing half of Team Sputnik, and has also collaborated with other artists in the *Graphic Classics* volumes *Edgar Allan Poe, Arthur Conan Doyle, H. G. Wells, Jack London, Ambrose Bierce, O. Henry, Rafael Sabatini, Horror Classics, Adventure Classics* and *Gothic Classics.*

NICK MILLER *(page 75)*

Nick was born and raised in the depths of rural England, and now lives in Lancaster, UK with his partner, Antonella Caputo. The son of two artists, he learned to draw at an early age. After leaving art school he worked as a graphic designer before switching to cartooning and illustration full-time in the early '90s. Since then his work has appeared in many comics and magazines in the UK, US and Europe, as well as in comic anthologies, websites and in advertising. His weekly comic strip, *The Really Heavy Greatcoat*, can be seen online at www.lancasterukonline.net. He works as part of Team Sputnik with Antonella Caputo, and also independently with other writers including John Freeman, Tony Husband, Mark Rogers and Tim Quinn. Nick's stories have appeared in *Graphic Classics: Arthur Conan Doyle*, *Graphic Classics: H.G. Wells*, *Graphic Classics: Ambrose Bierce*, *Graphic Classics: Jack London*, *Horror Classics* and *Adventure Classics*.

WILLIAM L. BROWN *(pages 1, 90)*

Political cartoonist and illustrator William L. Brown is the author of *President Bill, A Graphic Epic*, and the continuing cartoon *Citizen Bill*. His illustration clients include *The Washington Post*, *The Wall Street Journal*, *Slate* online magazine, *The Los Angeles Times* and *The Progressive*. He works in scratchboard, digitally adding color and grey tones. He cites as influences William Morris, John Held, Jr., and the British cartoonist Giles. Bill lives in Takoma Park, Maryland, a suburb of Washington, D.C., with his wife and two children. See more of his work in *Graphic Classics: Ambrose Bierce*, and at www.wmlbrown.com.

SIMON GANE *(page 94)*

British artist Simon Gane lives and works in Bath as a magazine and children's book illustrator and graphic designer. His first published strips appeared in the self-produced punk fanzine *Arnie*, and others followed in self-contained mini comics and eventually the collection *Punk Strips*. He recently completed *All Flee*, a comic about a "finishing school for monsters" and a four-issue series set in the Paris and New York of the 1950s for Slave Labor Graphics. "I especially enjoyed drawing *The Policeman and the Citizen* in *Graphic Classics: Ambrose Bierce*," says Simon, "because it encompasses many of my favorite themes: alcohol, police aggression, a past-times setting and a sense that whilst largely forgotten now, comics remain a peerless medium for satire." For *Is He Living or Is He Dead?* Simon spent time sketching in Menton, the setting of the story, which contributes to the rich backgrounds and detail that are also evident in his interpretations of *The Engineer's Thumb* for *Graphic Classics: Arthur Conan Doyle*, *The Invisible Man* for *Graphic Classics: H.G. Wells*, *The Shadow Over Innsmouth* for *Graphic Classics: H.P. Lovecraft* and *Dr. Jekyll and Mr. Hyde* for *Graphic Classics: Robert Louis Stevenson*.

RICK GEARY *(page 106)*

Rick is best known for his thirteen years as a contributor to *The National Lampoon*. His work has also appeared in Marvel, DC, and Dark Horse comics, *Rolling Stone*, *Mad*, *Heavy Metal*, *Disney Adventures*, *The Los Angeles Times*, and *The New York Times Book Review*. He is a regular cartoonist in *Rosebud*. Rick has written and illustrated five children's books and published a collection of his comics, *Housebound with Rick Geary*. The ninth volume in his continuing book series *A Treasury of Victorian Murder* is *The Bloody Benders* (NBM Publishing). More of Rick's work has appeared in the *Graphic Classics* anthologies *Edgar Allan Poe*, *Arthur Conan Doyle*, *H.G. Wells*, *Ambrose Bierce*, *H.P. Lovecraft* and *O. Henry*. You can also view his art at www.rickgeary.com.

TOM POMPLUN

The designer, editor and publisher of *Graphic Classics*, Tom has a background in commercial art and magazine publishing and a lifelong interest in comics. He designed and produced *Rosebud*, a journal of fiction, poetry and illustration, from 1993 to 2003, and in 2001 he founded *Graphic Classics*. Tom is currently working on *Fantasy Classics: Graphic Classics Volume 15*, scheduled for March 2008 release. The book will feature a new comics adaptation of Mary Shelley's *Frankenstein*, scripted by Rod Lott and painted by Skot Olsen. Plus H.P. Lovecraft's epic fantasy *The Dream Quest of Unknown Kadath*, by Ben Avery and Malaysian illustrator Leong Wan Kok, and "Oz" author L. Frank Baum's *The Glass Dog*, by Antonella Caputo and Brad Teare. Also Nathaniel Hawthorne's *Rappaccini's Daughter*, adapted by Lance Tooks, and *After the Fire*, a poem by fantasy master Lord Dunsany, illustrated by Rachel Masilamani. With a dramatic cover painting by Skot Olsen.

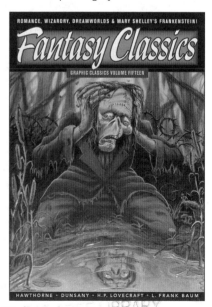